Inside Trading

Set in Battenberg's, an ancient London merchant bank with a proud tradition and a suspect past, *Inside Trading* centres on a rogue trader whose ambitions for his own survival draw in government, European funding and our millennial dreams.

Malcolm Bradbury is a novelist, critic, television dramatist and Emeritus Professor of American Studies at the University of East Anglia. He is the author of six novels: *Eating People is Wrong* (1959); *Stepping Westward* (1965); *The History Man* (1975), which won the Royal Society of Literature Heinemann Prize and was adapted for television; *Rates of Exchange* (1983), which was shortlisted for the Booker Prize; *Cuts: A Very Short Novel* (1987) and *Doctor Criminale* (1992). His critical works include *The Modern American Novel* (1984, revised 1992), *No, Not Bloomsbury* (essays, 1987), *The Modern World: Ten Great Writers* (1989), *From Puritanism to Postmodernism: A History of American Literature* (with Richard Ruland, 1993) and *The Modern British Novel* (1994). He has also edited *The Penguin Book of Modern British Short Stories* (1988), *Modernism* (with James McFarlane, 1991), *Dangerous Pilgrimages* (1995) and *The Atlas of Literature* (1996). He is the author of *Who Do You Think You Are?* (1993), a collection of seven stories and nine parodies, and of several works of humour and satire, including *Why Come to Slaka?* (1992), *Unsent Letters* (revised edition, 1995), *Mensonge* (1993). He has written several television 'novels' including *The Gravy Train* and *The Gravy Train Goes East*, has adapted other works for television including Tom Sharpe's *Porterhouse Blue*, Kingsley Amis's *The Green Man*, Stella Gibbons's *Cold Comfort Farm* (also released as a feature film) and written episodes of *A Touch of Frost* and *Dalziel and Pascoe*. In 1991, he was awarded the CBE.

by the same author

fiction
Eating People is Wrong
Stepping Westward
The History Man
The After Dinner Game: Three Plays for Television
Rate of Exchange
Why Come to Slaka?
Cuts
Doctor Criminale

criticism
Possibilities: Essays on the State of the Novel
Modernism (*editor, with J.W. McFarlane*)
The Novel Today (*editor*)
All Dressed Up and Nowhere to Go
The Modern American Novel
Saul Bellow
The Penguin Book of Modern British Short Stories
(*editor*)
No, Not Bloomsbury
Unsent Letters
Mensonge
From Puritanism to Postmodernism: A History of
American Literature (*with Richard Ruland*)
The Modern British Novel
Dangerous Pilgrimages

INSIDE TRADING

a comedy in three acts

by **Malcolm Bradbury**

heavily adapted from the play

JUGEND VORAN or HO-RUCK

by **Paul Vulpius**

Methuen Drama

A Methuen Modern Play

First published in this edition in 1997 by Methuen Drama

Copyright © 1997 by Malcolm Bradbury
Introduction copyright © 1997 by Malcolm Bradbury

Malcolm Bradbury has asserted his right
under the Copyright, Designs and Patents Act, 1988
to be identified as the author of this work

Published in the United Kingdom in 1997 by Methuen
Random House, 20 Vauxhall Bridge Road, London SW1V 2SA

Random House Australia (Pty) Limited
20 Alfred Street, Milsons Point, Sydney,
New South Wales 2061, Australia

Random House New Zealand Limited
18 Poland Road, Glenfield,
Auckland 10, New Zealand

Random House South Africa (Pty) Limited
Endulini, 5a Jubilee Road, Parktown 2193, South Africa

Distributed in the United States of America by Heinemann,
a division of Reed Elsevier Inc. 361 Hanover Street, Portsmouth,
New Hampshire NH 03801 3959

Random House UK Limited Reg. No. 954009

Extracts from *All That Glitters: The Fall of Barings* reproduced by
permission of John Gapper

A CIP catalogue record for this book is available
from the British Library

ISBN 0 413 71740 2

Typeset by Wilmaset Ltd, Birkenhead, Wirral
Printed and bound in Great Britain by
Cox & Wyman Ltd, Reading, Berkshire

Caution

Introduction

Inside Trading – which is a satirical comedy for the 1990s – was stirred into existence by a German play from the 1930s. This is a play with an interesting and decidedly curious history. *Jugend Voran, Or Ho-Ruck*, by Paul Vulpius, was first performed in Berlin in the autumn of 1933. This was a rather surprising year for the staging of a new comedy. At the beginning of 1933, it will be recalled, Adolf Hitler was appointed Reichschancellor, after an uneasy and violent election had produced an unstable coalition government. Post-war Germany had twice been ravaged by economic depression: once in the early 1920s, under the burdens of war reparations imposed by the Versailles Treaty, when the mark slipped so badly that people pushed cartloads of them along the streets; and again now, at the heart of the deep world depression that followed the Wall Street Crash of 1929.

Once again banks started collapsing, and the mark turned to paper. In the meantime, during 1933, and especially following the mysterious Reichstag Fire in the spring, the Nazis used every means to consolidate their power. Christopher Isherwood, that famous literary camera, vividly captures the change from the impoverished but hectic and often creative decadence of the Weimar period to the rising totalitarian mood of the early 1930s. 'Berlin was in a state of civil war . . .' he writes in *Mr Norris Changes Trains* (1939). 'Hate exploded suddenly, without warning, out of nowhere; at street corners, in restaurants, cinemas, dance-halls, swimming baths; at midnight, after breakfast, in the middle of the afternoon . . . Frl. Schroeder's astrologer foretold the end of the world . . .'

It was a year of persecution and cultural terror. Great piles of forbidden books were burned in the market-places of German cities. The works of authors – Jewish, German, foreign – disliked by the Nazis were banned. A whole generation of writers, including such distinguished figures as Thomas Mann (who had lately won the Nobel Prize for Literature) and, in theatre, Bertolt Brecht, were driven into exile, many to pursue their careers in Hollywood. Some became Nazi supporters, others were silenced, some committed suicide.

This was the climate in which *Jugend Voran* was staged, at the Theater in der Behrenstrasse in Berlin, opening on 24 October 1933. It is (if the phrase isn't an oxymoron) a German farce, about a time of economic troubles. Like most good farce, it is based round one simple and excellent idea. A persuasive young man with everything except a job tricks his way into the weary bureaucracy of a musty, dusty old bank, a Kafkaesque institution where clerks ply their pens, paper is exchanged, and nothing ever gets done. He changes everything: does some trading, invents a major new project, charms everyone, wins over the banker's daughter, and seems to restore not just the fortunes of a single bank but economic hopes about the future.

It's partly a romantic comedy, so the young lovers win over the old guard. In fact the title means something like *Youth to the Fore*, and the subtitle something like *Heave Ho*. But it's also a serious satirical farce, and, appropriately enough, given the times, the message appears to be just a little obscure. On the one hand, everyone's fortunes do seem about to improve; but this has been achieved corruptly. If the bank itself is a bit like old Germany, the rogue hero is the symbol of the new generation. And if it seems the young might be able to put things right after all, it's not exactly clear which new and energetic group of youth (it is hard not to forget that by this time there was, after all, the Hitler Youth in the background) is putting its hand to the plough.

As far as the few German reviews of the play I've seen are concerned, it seems to have been received chiefly as a romantic comedy, offering some light relief for the troubled season, rather than as a political tract. The play was performed and published again in Vienna in the following year. But now the names of the bank and of some of the characters have changed, and the social attitudes seem rather different. It then appeared in London in a very light-hearted British adaptation by Hubert Griffith, the playwright, drama critic and author of books on Russia. It opened at the Globe Theatre on 20 February 1934, with a starry cast that included Alistair Sim, Kay Hammond, and the matinée idol and film star Owen Nares, and ran with considerable success.

So far, and after various industrious researches, I still have been unable to find out much about the original author, Paul Vulpius: who he was, what became of him. Given the circumstances of the day and the way theatre worked, I have not been able to avoid the suspicion that the author's name is an elegant pseudonym, and some unknown other lies at the back of it all. For the Berlin version (but not the Viennese) a second author with an Anglo-Saxon name is mentioned: Ralph Arthur Roberts. No doubt further research will remove this ignorance, and various authorities are working at it. But information so far has not been easy to find.

The Vulpius play was first brought to my attention by Henry Burke, the energetic founder of the new Norwich Playhouse, which opened its fine new doors at the old Gun Wharf, on the banks of the River Wensum, in 1995. He'd remembered the British production from a post-war radio adaptation, and set out to trace down the original German and Austrian versions: something he duly managed to do. I at once shared his fascination – and not only because I was intrigued by the not entirely familiar idea of a German farce. Perhaps, and more probably, the play will turn out originally to have been an Austrian farce, for Vienna of course has a much stronger tradition of stage comedy.

Nor was it only because I thought it was cunningly constructed, with an excellent idea at the centre, and a fast-developing set of complications, a great gift for the comic turning of the screw. I found myself particularly fascinated by the central figure – a splendid version of that familiar anti-hero of the nineties: the Rogue Trader. Rogue traders are not new. They abound throughout literature; Charles Dickens and Anthony Trollope, Herman Melville and Mark Twain, Thomas Mann and Robert Musil were fascinated by the similar defaulting personalities and confidence men of their own day. But given recent events in the world of banking, Vulpius's story had in it a surprisingly and glorious topicality. So the idea of a radical adaptation was born.

We first commissioned, from Brenda Ferris, a flat literal translation of the original published text, which served as the foundation for this present play. It is, indeed, a radical adaptation – firmly transposed across the historic space of sixty years in which the world and the century have totally changed. The Germany of the thirties was a place of world depression, a falling mark, political crisis, rising totalitarianism, deep ideological conflict between the Nazis and the Communists, and emerging fears of war. *Inside Trading* of course belongs to the age of global trading, offshore corporations, plastic money, screen-based dealing, electronic commodities, futures and derivatives, rampant commercialism, tiger economies, and a post-ideological, post-Cold War, post-modern world culture, based on image, lifestyle, greed and shopping.

In our own present world, banks collapse not because of the failure of the capitalist world economy, but because of its intercontinental success. There are Big Bangs leading to Small Crashes, Lucky Fridays turning into Black Mondays, a bull for every bear. But the systems of trading are so international, speedy, inventive and technological that every failure usually proves to be someone else's success. High-rise financial towers rise up in phallic competition over every major trading city. Money knows no borders, the exchanges of the world trade over a full twenty-four hours. New kinds of trading, new forms of commodity, new brands of money, new types of transaction are invented all the time, so the old banking system strains at the seams.

A spectacular example of the new market-place was to be, of course, the collapse of Barings in London in February 1995. In their fascinating book on that subject, *All That Glitters: The Fall of Barings* (1996), John Gapper and Nicholas Denton tell this sad, very British tale in fine detail, and draw some useful lessons. In modern times, these distinguished and gentlemanly merchant banks, with their mahogany boardrooms and their beadles, have been highly regarded for their prudence. In fact in the past they had often been among the greatest risk-takers. Typically enough of such institutions, Barings was founded in 1763 by a German family from Bremen. They became international bankers, supported both sides in the Napoleonic Wars, funded the American Louisiana Purchase in 1803 (one of the great bargains of history, when Thomas Jefferson bought half the North American continent from a preoccupied Napoleon), financed British imperial expansion, and got involved in railroad and development schemes across the Americas.

Barings had collapsed once before, in the 1890s, as a result of holding unstable investments in the Buenos Aires water and sewage system, which remains no great shakes to this day. (At an earlier date, in the 1840s, Argentina had actually offered Barings the Malvinas (the Falkland Islands) to settle a defaulting loan.) But in those days bankers saved their own. The institution was rescued by Bank of England and rival bankers, relaunched and redirected, and set on its distinguished course in the twentieth century.

Like many writers (in fact like most people who had a little money to invest), Charles Dickens had a very ironic view of private banking in his own Victorian times. And no wonder, for many of these investors lost their savings and annuities in various schemes, bubbles and illusory Edens abroad, or offshore, and not least in American banks and railroads. It was Dickens who invented the phrase 'the Almighty Dollar' as a warning to those who put too much trust in American promissory notes. But the banks in England were no better, and Dickens always had a far from trusting attitude to the creators of trust, a speculative attitude to the makers of speculations.

'Within the offices were newly plastered, newly painted, newly papered, newly countered, newly floor-clothed, newly tabled, newly chaired, newly fitted up in every way, with goods that were substantial and expensive, and designed (like the company) to last . . .' he writes in the 1840s (a bad time for banking, for this was when the Almighty Dollar was proving a good deal less than mighty) in *Martin Chuzzlewit*, of one of his best inventions, the Anglo-Bengalee Bank. The institution – very different, let me say, from Barings – is run as an impressive deception by a certain Mr Montague Tigg. He explains his system: 'Is that a crowded street . . . ?' he asks, 'I can tell you how many of 'em will buy annuities, effect insurances, bring us their money in a hundred shapes and ways, force it upon us, trust us as if we were the Mint; yet know no more about us than you do of that crossing-sweeper on the corner.'

That was the Victorian attitude to banks and banking, reinforced again in *Little Dorrit* and Trollope's *The Way We Live Now*. But in the present century the image changed. The older and more enduring of the merchant banks increasingly came to represent caution, prudence, the solid, traditional, reliable and trustworthy face of the famous London Square Mile, so different from banking abroad. Their boardrooms were splendid, their dining-rooms gratifying, their clients distinguished if not royal, their manners discreet, their bank servants and beadles civil, their word was their bond. Then, in the still amazing era of Mrs Thatcher – who for all her conservative reputation was never exactly a friend to entrenched and traditional institutions – Big Bang opened up the City to deregulation, to high-flying American investment banks with their new ways.

The Big Bang pushed the merchant banks into taking on the roles of jobbing and brokering, and into massive trading on the competitive, screen-based international exchanges – roles to which they were hardly well-suited or in which they were very experienced. New banking types emerged – above all the high-flying star traders, the Big Swinging Dicks, shifting millions, competing with each other for salaries and bonuses. New screen-based dealing rooms, computer links and forms of post-paper trading and arbitraging developed in complicated synergies right across the world. Adrenalin drove dealing; young dealers battled to be masters or mistresses of the universe. Back offices were swamped. Sales of champagne, Porsche cars, red braces, shirts by Pink and mobile phones rose rapidly. The age of the yuppie was born.

As *All That Glitters* points out to us, the 1990s was to become the decade of 'the Rogue Trader', a striking, if in many ways rather convenient, phenomenon. The smaller, private, merchant banks had had to go into trading to compensate for declining profits elsewhere: 'Those without adequate controls had to trust young men and women whom they paid highly to buy and sell financial contracts that were too complex for most managers to understand. It left them vulnerable to being deceived on a grand scale.' They also note that the traders themselves frequently did not gain personally through their deceptions, except in inflated bonuses: 'They appeared instead to have drifted into deception in an effort to be seen as star traders. In each case the "star trader" was quickly disowned when the effort collapsed. The institutions that had paid them large sums and praised them for their extraordinary feats in financial markets condemned them as "rogue traders".' As a result, few of the merchant banks – often themselves German in origin, financiers of princelings and European wars, yet somehow symbols of a traditional core of British culture and gentlemanly dealing – have survived intact, any more than has the culture for which they stood.

So, turned round from a story of the troubled and totalitarian thirties, *Inside Trading* developed in my mind as a story of the post-ideological and nervous nineties. It's certainly not intended to be about Barings, and I began work on the play well ahead of their unhappy disaster. No, this was to be a satirical, farcical comedy about the shifting, transforming Square Mile and the dawning, dream-filled, scheme-filled Millennium, about the new, laddish, wine-bar-fuelled, high-flying risk-taking age of Post-modern Youth to the Fore. My version is thus a fairly hefty step away from Paul Vulpius's Berlin play of sixty years ago.

But I am heartily grateful to our half-hidden Vulpius for his original stagecraft, wonderful central idea, light-hearted vision, and cunning plot: even if I have chosen to settle it in rather a different – a less romantic and affirmative – way. And I am especially grateful to Henry Burke, not just for so enthusiastically putting the original text of the play in front of me and commissioning an adaptation, but for directing the premiere production at the Norwich Playhouse from 28

November to 14 December 1996. I am also grateful to the strong and very helpful cast, who added their own ideas, and the striking set design by David Jewell. I am grateful too for Brenda Ferris's translation, which provided the scaffolding that let this fictional bank building arise, and no doubt eventually fall, and for David Cargill's advice on banking. I hope the play still gives its farcical pleasure, and will make its point. In the meantime, any further information about Paul Vulpius would be very gratefully received.

Malcolm Bradbury, 1997

INSIDE TRADING

To Jessica
who nearly came to the first night

Inside Trading was first performed at the Norwich Playhouse on 28 November 1996, with the following cast:

Tim Wickerman	Duncan Wisbey
'Frog' Froggatt	Jonathan Roby
Sir Richard Battenberg	Richard Heffer
Beadle	Vince Hadley
Maybelle	Kirsten May
Helga	Amanda Nolan
Hartley Fenton	Christopher Scoular
Lord Holbeck	Peter Whitbread
Paston-Jones	Eugene Williams
Jurgen Fabry/Journalist	Stephen Ley
Mortimer Fitzroy/Journalist	Jonathan Rea
Old Man	Barrie Hesketh

Directed by Henry Burke
Designed by David Jewell

Characters

Tim Wickerman, *a young man of promise*
'Frog' Froggatt, *a Banker's PA*
Sir Richard Battenberg, *Chairman of Battenberg's Bank*
Bank Beadle (*Mr Bennett*)
Maybelle, *a private secretary*
Helga, *Sir Richard's daughter*
Hartley Fenton, *the Bank's CEO*
Lord Holbeck, *a Bank partner*
Paston-Jones, *the Bank's Deputy Chairman*
Jurgen Fabry, *another Banker*
Mortimer Fitzroy, *a Junior Minister*
Old Man
Two **Journalists**

Setting

The action takes place in the Chairman's suite at Battenberg's Bank in the City of London. The time is the present.

Act One

A morning in summer.

The top-floor executive suite at Battenberg's Bank, in the heart of the City of London. It's one of the proudest and oldest of the merchant banks, and evidently prides itself on keeping up those grand old City traditions. We see mahogany walls and a gleaming conference table toward the rear of the stage. There are old banking portraits, hunting pictures and pictures of sailing clippers hung. But there are many signs that the age of computers and dealing screens has affected and modernized the bank. Suspended monitors and time clocks show flickering information about world markets.

This is the entrance area to the Chairman's suite. A corridor backstage is visible, as through a glass wall; it has the glass door to the suite in it. Off the suite are two wooden doors with signs on them. They say CHAIRMAN and CHAIRMAN'S SECRETARY. Centre stage is a reception desk where the Chairman's Executive Secretary works. It has a desktop computer, and the user's name on the desk, Mr Peter Froggatt. There is a dignified leather sofa for visitors to sit on, and a gleaming conference table in the background.

*Before lights come up and the action starts, we might hear over the sound system Mrs Thatcher's speech during the 1980s, praising the bright young men of the age of City deregulation. The phone in the secretary's office rings. It stops, then the call resumes on **Froggatt**'s desk. It stops as . . .*

*The lift bell pings, and in the corridor the **Beadle** – a stout middle-aged man dressed in the kind of uniform beadles at the Bank of England wear, top hat and braided coat – appears with a bunch of keys. He's followed by **Froggatt**, who is a gangling young man in his twenties. He wears a cycling helmet and various city cyclist's equipment: luminous warning strips and so on. He carries a bicycle wheel in his hand. The **Beadle** unlocks the door for him, holds it open, follows him in.*

Beadle   There we go, Mr Froggatt. In early this morning.

Froggatt   I'm in early every morning.

Beadle   True enough, sir. First to arrive, last to leave. Bank wouldn't seem half as busy without you.

Froggatt *is removing his cycling impedimenta. He puts it all carefully away, including the bike wheel, in the wardrobe. He gradually emerges from this transformation as a latter-day yuppie: baggy suit, Turnbull and Asser shirt, red motor-racing braces.*

Froggatt   I like to be early. I like to feel when I start the day I . . . really start the day. Is there a clean towel in the lavatory?

Beadle   That I don't know, sir. Don't do towels. Not part of my duties. Security, that's what they pay me for. And dressing up like a silly bugger, of course.

The phone rings again on **Froggatt**'s *desk.*

Phone's ringing, sir.

Froggatt *doesn't answer it.*

Froggatt   I know. Today's chairman's day. Sir Richard always likes a fresh towel.

Beadle   Still, I'm proud of it, to tell the truth, sir. Top hat and braid's always been a tradition for the beadles at Battenberg's Bank.

Froggatt   Well, it's a very traditional place, isn't it?

Beadle   Nothing wrong with that. Look around some of the other banks in the Square Mile. You'll see guards in security uniform like blooming vigilantes. Coshes, some of them have. That's the kind of world we live in. Mace and stun guns. But that is not, and has never been, the Battenberg spirit.

Froggatt *goes to his desk. The phone stops ringing.*

Froggatt   Quite right. Definitely not.

Beadle   Pension fraud. Drug laundering. Rogue trading. Insider dealing. All these young kids of dealers from Chingford, always on about futures. I say there's no point in thinking about futures if you can't remember the past.

Froggatt Market forces, Mr Bennett. It's a global economy. Look at it up there. Frankfurt. Wall Street. Then the Nikkei, the Hang Seng. Money doesn't sleep any more. It goes on day and night.

Beadle That's not money, is it? It's little chips. But if you ask me, that shouldn't change Battenberg's. Battenberg's always been more a gentleman's club. And I'm more a gentleman's gentleman. You did look in the gentlemen's, did you, sir?

Froggatt No, I didn't look in the gentleman's. Sir Richard will have to scrub himself clean with a paper towel for once.

The phone rings again.

Beadle Phone's ringing again, sir.

Froggatt I know, I know. This is my quality time. We're not in working hours yet. That's everything, Bennett.

Beadle Very well, Mr Froggatt.

The **Beadle** *goes.* **Froggatt** *goes and sits down at his elegant desk. He stares at the phone; it stops ringing. He opens a drawer, gets out a duster, and scrupulously polishes the top. Then he takes out two dumbbells. He does push-ups with them for a moment. He pushes back his chair and indulges in some posture exercises, which begin with rapid head turning and progress into sweeping movements with his body, from side to side.* **Maybelle**, *a young and personable secretary, comes in through the door. She stops and stares at* **Froggatt**.

Maybelle Morning, Mr Froggatt. That what you do when no one's watching? Have a nice little work-out?

Froggatt *stops.*

Froggatt You're in early, Maybelle.

Maybelle *hangs up her coat.*

Maybelle No bomb alert for once, was there? What are you up to then? Princess Diana invite you out?

Froggatt These are desk-based exercises recommended by leading body counsellors. To minimize executive stress.

Maybelle   They teach you to do it on aeroplanes now.
Well, it's better than shagging in the loos.

She comes over to **Froggatt***'s desk.*

Go out raving round the clubs last night, Mr Froggatt?

Froggatt   No, I didn't. I stayed in and watched the
snooker.

Maybelle   It's just a lot of balls to me.

Froggatt   Yes, well, I love it because it's so clean and
abstract. Just like mobile Mondrian.

Maybelle   I had a sushi and went to a disco. You should
party more, Froggie.

Froggatt   Oh yes. When did that become a verb?

Maybelle   When did which become a what?

Froggatt   Party happens to be a noun. So when did it
become a verb? To party. I party, you party. They will
party. We have partied.

Maybelle   Sounds fun to me. I just know you ought to get
out more. People will start thinking you're a trainspotter.
Listen, I heard an interesting rumour last night.

Froggatt   What?

Maybelle   Someone in the Bank's been insider trading.

The phone rings again.

Froggatt   That's the phone ringing, Maybelle.

Maybelle   I know. And that's my office I'm in.

Maybelle *goes off within.* **Froggatt** *answers the phone.*

Froggatt   Battenberg's Bank, Chairman's office . . . No,
the Chairman isn't in yet . . . No, the Vice-Chairman isn't in
either . . . No, nor is the Chief Executive . . . Well, this is a
merchant bank, not an all-night filling station . . . I'm sorry,
sir, I didn't realize you were the Governor of the Bank of
England . . . Well, no one's in. Except me, I'm in . . . The
Chairman's personal assistant. Oh. Same to you then.

The lift pings. **Froggatt** *looks at the phone and puts it down. He looks up. Someone is tapping on the glass door. It's* **Tim Wickerman**, *twenties, seemingly well-dressed, though a touch, as they say, distressed.* **Froggatt** *shakes his head.* **Wickerman** *nods his.* **Froggatt** *makes a negative gesture with his hands.*
Wickerman *puts his hands to his heart.* **Froggatt** *gets up and goes and opens the door.*

Froggatt   Sorry, sir. Nobody's allowed up here. This is the top floor.

Wickerman (*looks round*)   So it is. But you're here, aren't you?

Froggatt   Yes, I know I'm here. But I'm personal assistant to the Chairman, and only senior executives and directors are permitted on the top floor. This is sacred space. You should never have been allowed up here.

Wickerman   I must have pressed the wrong button in the lift.

Froggatt   There is no button in the lift. It's the partners' lift.

Wickerman   So I got in the wrong lift.

Froggatt   Would you kindly get in it again and go down?

Wickerman (*stares*)   Hang on! It's Frog, isn't it? Froggie Froggatt?

Froggatt (*nervous*)   What do you mean?

Wickerman   Felsted School, 1982 to 88. It's Tim Wickerman. Remember, I was captain of rugby. You ran the stamp club. Personal assistant to Sir Richard Battenberg? Haven't you done nicely, Froggie?

Froggatt   Please don't call me Froggie. I never did like it.

Wickerman *has come centre stage.*

Wickerman   The trouble is, you are Froggie. I mean, the whole world knows you're Froggie.

Froggatt   No, they don't, Wickerman.

Wickerman   Glorious office like this. No partitions.
Smoke if you like. Who would have guessed it? And you used
to be such a little nerd.

Froggatt   I was not a little nerd. Now please go, I'm busy.

Wickerman   I bet you are. Froggie Froggatt, always busy.
Still, now he's chief assistant to the assistant chief.

Wickerman *sits at* **Froggatt**'*s desk*.

Froggatt   Wickerman, that's my chair you're sitting in.

Wickerman   I presume even an assistant chief is allowed
to entertain his friends from school?

Froggatt   I never thought of you as a friend, Wickerman.
You stole my tuck. Made me write your essays.

Wickerman   But that's how the greatest friendships are
made, Frog. It's called male bonding. Friendships that go on
for a lifetime. Last through thick and thin. Good and bad.
Rain and shine. That's how Marks met Spencer. Reckitt met
Colman. Tie met Rack.

Froggatt   How did you find out I worked here?

Wickerman   Funnily enough, I didn't. It's just a strange
piece of cosmic good fortune I met you again.

Froggatt   Oh no, it isn't.

Wickerman   Not for you. For me, I mean.

Froggatt   You were a rotten bully at school, Wickerman.
Do you know that?

Wickerman   I suppose I did know that. Boys are clever,
aren't they? And the funny thing is, Frog – I still am.

Froggatt *looks at him nervously*.

Froggatt   Just go, Wickerman. Top floor's a financially
sensitive area. Or I'll call Mr Bennett the Beadle.

Wickerman *swivels in the chair and looks around*.

Wickerman   This is really nice, Frog. Look at those
portraits. All the Old Fartonians in their wigs and

stovepipes. There's the Wreck of the Hesperus. And just look at this lovely desk. Does someone come in early every morning and give it a very special polish?

Froggatt Yes. I do.

Wickerman Of course, Frog. Now honestly. Red braces. Didn't anyone ever tell you the eighties are over? They pulled down the Berlin Wall? Mrs Thatcher resigned? The cows went mad? Now we're into ties, Frog. Italian silk. Jeremy Paxman ties.

He stares up at the screens.

Don't care very much for the look of the Hang Seng, do you?

Froggatt You're not a dealer, are you, Wickerman?

Wickerman No. Not yet.

Froggatt Not . . . yet?

Wickerman You're lucky to have caught me. I was just making my way round a few of the top merchant banks.

Froggatt So you are in banking?

Wickerman No, I just thought banks were where the money was. It's a kind of logical connection. No, at the moment I'm working for the government. I've joined their downsizing programme. I've been naturally wasted. Heard of the feel-bad factor? Executive unemployment, the problem of the nineties. You've read the articles. Now meet the man himself.

Froggatt What, you mean you're unemployed?

Wickerman That's it. How would you feel about a jobshare, Froggie?

Froggatt I . . . don't know what you mean.

Wickerman The government's granted me a great deal of free time lately. So I've been onlining.

Froggatt There's no such verb as to online.

Wickerman   There is now. And I decided to access the files of Battenberg's Bank.

Froggatt   Or to access. You did what?

Wickerman   I see you're still a nerd, Frog. Well, thanks to the Pentium processor there's nothing at all I don't know about this business. How many staff have you got here? Go on, guess.

Froggatt   Look, I've no time to . . .

Wickerman   Come on, Frog.

Froggatt   Oh, two hundred.

Wickerman   Three twenty-seven. Including overseas.

Froggatt   Fascinating.

Wickerman   Which makes me wonder who could possibly notice one more. Is this nice desk your desk, Frog?

Froggatt   Oh no, Wickerman.

Wickerman   Look, Frog, I'll give you a fair choice. Either I keep this desk, or you call equipment for another one and we'll put it over there.

Froggatt   No. Why would I do that?

Wickerman   Remember Felsted. Old boys stick together. I'd do exactly the same for you.

Froggatt   You're round the twist, Wickerman. The first person who came into the office would want to know who the hell you were.

Wickerman   Let's test that, shall we? (*He picks up the phone.*) Hello, my dear, could you ask Mr Bennett to come up to the Chairman's suite? Thanks. How's your mother? Is she really? Oh, good.

He puts down the phone. **Froggatt** *stares at him.*

Froggatt   How did you know she had a mother?

Wickerman   I work on the crude principle that most people do.

Froggatt Wickerman, I want you out of here. At once.

Wickerman OK, maybe you'll get your wish. Maybe ten minutes from now I'll be chucked out on my bottom line. But why not give it a sporting chance? You always liked a flutter at Felsted, Frog.

Froggatt No, I didn't. I hate gambling.

Wickerman Well, have a go now. Remember, it could be you.

Froggatt Look, Wickers, you won't be the one who suffers. I could lose my job for even letting you come up here. This is back office. This is the inner sanctum.

*The **Beadle** comes in.*

Beadle You called me, Mr Froggatt?

Froggatt No, I didn't, Mr Bennett.

Beadle There was a bleep on my bleepyphone . . .

Wickerman Morning, Mr Bennett. How's the wife today?

Beadle Not too good at all, sir. They say they want to keep her in a bit longer.

Wickerman Tests? Awful, isn't it? We really ought to try and find you a few hours off, didn't we? So you can go and take her Pot Noodles or something.

Beadle Be a big help, sir, I can tell you that.

Wickerman I'll raise it with Sir Richard pronto. And we'll see what we can do.

Beadle Thank you, sir.

Wickerman Oh by the way, Bennett. If anyone asks for me, just tell them I've been shifted upstairs to work here with the senior executive team.

*The **Beadle** looks at him, mystified.*

Beadle Yes, sir, but . . .

Wickerman   Mr Wickerman! You'd not forgotten, had you, Mr Bennett?

Beadle   No, course not, Mr Wickerman, but . . .

Wickerman   Oh, Bennett, for some reason they've forgotten to put a desk for me in here. Would you nip over to equipment and have one sent over soonest?

Beadle   Right you are, Mr Wickerman. Sorry, sir, I forget which department were you in before?

Wickerman   Futures and Options.

Beadle   Course, that's it, sir.

Wickerman   Before that in Ventures. Before that in Risks.

Beadle   I knew you'd been with us for a while, sir, but . . .

Wickerman   Oh, and I ought to have a desktop computer. A dealing screen. State of the art. If not better.

Beadle   Just leave it with me, Mr Wickerman.

Wickerman   I will. Couldn't be in better hands, could it?

Beadle   Do believe you're right there, sir.

The **Beadle** *goes, plainly gratified.* **Wickerman** *looks up at* **Froggatt**.

Wickerman   Well, what do you think, Frog?

Froggatt   What do I think? I think you're a total bloody bastard, Wickerman. You can intimidate me . . .

Wickerman   I know I can. Back of the bike-sheds, Froggie.

Froggatt   . . . You can fool the Beadle. But just you wait till the Chairman comes in.

Wickerman   I can't wait to see the Chairman. Sir Richard Battenberg, you mean?

Froggatt   You can't wait?

Wickerman I should say, see him again. I've been chatting him up for weeks. Covent Garden. *Les Misérables*. Wimbledon. Lords. Guildhall Banquets.

Froggatt Guildhall Banquets? How the hell do you get to Guildhall Banquets? You're bloody unemployed.

Wickerman Yes, Frog, but you don't understand the nature of modern unemployment. Look at me. I may be on benefit, but I wear Armani. I may live in a squat, but I haven't stopped going to smart parties. It's the thing about London. I always think a man with a DJ never need starve in the summer.

Froggatt Parties?

Wickerman The fact is, I live very nicely on champagne and caviar nibbles. Go along to book launches, film previews, art openings. If you turn up, and you're not wearing a balaclava and carrying a Kalashnikov, they never turn you away. In fact at most art openings you could be hefting a rocket launcher. And they'd just call you punk post-modern and stuff the smoked salmon down your throat.

Froggatt But not at a Guildhall Banquet.

Wickerman No, not at a Guildhall Banquet. They have a marked seating plan there. The art's to go along for the drinks, but not miss out on the dinner. I'll say this for Sir Richard, he's a natural gentleman. Shy but always friendly. No memory. I just hope he'll remember how often we've chatted on together at all these social functions.

Froggatt Have you?

Wickerman Yes, my mother's an old friend of his wife.

Froggatt Is she really?

Wickerman No. But as long as he thinks she is, she is.

Froggatt All right. It's one thing to meet Sir Richard over bubbly at some party. It's something else when you pop up right here in his private suite.

Wickerman   Let's see, shall we? The banking world changes so fast these days another new exec won't surprise him.

Froggatt   All he has to do is to check the payroll. And you're not there, are you?

Wickerman   Well, if I'm not on the payroll, I can't be downsized, can I? Not like you, Froggie.

Froggatt   And you can't be paid either.

Wickerman   I wasn't thinking of getting paid. Not at first anyway. I though I'd provide my services free.

Froggatt   What services?

Wickerman   You don't imagine I'd take a job in a bank unless I had a few ideas about investments, do you?

Froggatt   What ideas?

Wickerman   Trading. I want to get inside trading. Mind if I take a look?

He taps into the desk computer.

Froggatt (*great concern*)   Leave that alone. That's sacred. There are thousands of millions in share dealings in there.

Wickerman   Look, there's not much point in my working in the back office of Battenberg's unless I start wheeling in some business, is there? How do you buy and sell on this thing?

Froggatt   Wickers, no. No buying. And no selling.

Wickerman   Isn't there just a small account I could practise on? What's this, Kubinski Holdings? No share price quoted. Company dormant. Market closed.

Froggatt (*checking*)   That's because they've stopped trading. In fact they're technically bankrupt.

Wickerman   Good. That'll do for a start.

He taps into the computer.

Froggatt   What do you think you're doing?

Wickerman Making an offer on their shares.

Froggatt You can't trade on a dead account.

Wickerman Why not?

Froggatt Because you can't make bricks without straw.

Wickerman Course you can. People have been doing it for centuries. See, I've bought some. How about that?

Froggatt *checks the computer.*

Froggatt OK, you've found fifty worthless shares. What good's that?

Wickerman You'll see. Who is this bank's biggest rival?

Froggatt Jurgen Fabry. Why?

Wickerman Well, if I'm buying shares, I have to have someone to sell them to, don't I? I always understood that's how the market works.

Wickerman *keeps tapping the computer.*

Froggatt Please don't do anything to upset Jurgen Fabry. Anything.

Wickerman Why so concerned about Jurgen Fabry? I thought it was a cut-throat market-place. Blood over the wall.

Froggatt *looks at him in despair.*

Froggatt We don't want any blood over that wall. Not Jurgen Fabry. Stephen Fabry's engaged to Sir Richard's daughter. They're getting married in three weeks.

Wickerman Really?

Froggatt Present list at Harrod's. Wedding at St Margaret's, Westminster. Reception at the Oxo Tower. Honeymoon in the Seychelles.

Wickerman They want to trade their assets offshore, do they? It's all a bit old-fashioned, isn't it?

Froggatt   It's an old custom in banking. Uniting the great banking dynasties by marriage. It's what the Fuggers always used to do.

Wickerman   Really, Frog. You're getting very foul-mouthed in your old age.

Froggatt   And the Rothschilds and the Barings and the Warburgs and the Schroeders. Good business sense. It keeps the money in the family.

Maybelle *comes in, stares surprised at* **Wickerman**, *clearly running the shop*.

Maybelle   Well well, who are you?

Wickerman *rises as if stunned*.

Wickerman   Hullo, darling. I must say we're looking very attractive this morning.

Maybelle   Maybe we are and maybe we aren't, but who the hell are you? Come to fix the photocopier?

Wickerman   No, I'm Tim Wickerman from the Mortgage Department. I appear to have been elevated. Of course that feeling could just come from gazing at you.

Maybelle   Oh, yes? One of those?

Wickerman   And you are . . . ?

Maybelle   I'm Maybelle. The Chairman's secretary.

Wickerman   Well, now I'm in this office, I hope that means I'm entitled to full use of your services?

Maybelle   Secretarial maybe. And that's it.

Wickerman   Right then, Maybelle. Look, I seem to be computer-locked into Frankfurt at the moment. So would you mind calling Jurgen Fabry? Just ask for the chief honcho. And don't take no for an answer.

Maybelle   You mean Lord Fabry?

Wickerman That's the guy. And just tell him top floor at Battenberg's would like to know his latest angle on the Kubinski business.

Maybelle The Kubinski business?

Wickerman The Kubinski business. Play your cards close to that truly beautiful chest of yours. And whatever you do, don't give him a clue we're buying heavily.

Maybelle But are we?

Wickerman Oh God, are we? Kubinski's got to be the one. Body Shop of the nineties. Know what I mean?

Maybelle Sure. But we don't tell Lord Fabry that?

Wickerman No, that we do not do. What we're trying to do, as delicately as we can, is put him off. I know I can trust you. I can see you're a real player.

Maybelle Don't you want a chair, Mr Froggatt? You've nowhere to sit.

Froggatt I'm all right. Probably.

Wickerman No need to worry about Frog.

Maybelle *goes.* **Wickerman** *keeps tapping the computer.*

Froggatt Wickers. What's all that about?

Wickerman Just stirring up a bit of competitive interest. Somebody told me that's how capitalism works.

The lift pings. An elderly gentleman, respectable, appears in the corridor with a shoeshine stand and taps on the glass door.

Wickerman Frog, I thought you told me no one was allowed up here. Deal with that, would you?

Froggatt *goes to the door and opens it.*

Froggatt Sorry, sir, nobody's allowed up here.

Old Man I know, but I shine shoes on the trading floor. The young gentlemen have been very grateful. I thought you might care for some personal grooming as you worked, sir.

Froggatt   There is a sign on the lift. No admittance to visitors or unauthorized staff.

Old Man   Yes, sir, but in my day the first thing gentlemen bankers did in the morning was to have their shoes properly shined.

Froggatt   Look, not today, thank you. This is an international bank. Millions hang on our every minute. Go on, you heard . . .

The **Old Man** *goes.* **Wickerman** *turns to* **Froggatt**.

Wickerman   You know, Frog, you really can be awfully unpleasant when you don't try. Isn't it time we had a bit of civility up here?

Froggatt   What do you expect? You've taken my desk, you've taken my computer, you've taken my secretary. You're trading on my screen, you're buying shares, and now you're playing tricks on Jurgen Fabry. Oh, my God.

The lift pings. **Froggatt** *stares beyond the glass screen. The Chairman,* **Sir Richard Battenberg**, *a very distinguished gentleman dressed as for the country, has appeared and is tapping on the glass.* **Froggatt** *hurries to open the door.*

Froggatt   Good morning, Sir Richard.

Sir Richard *comes in.*

Sir Richard   Morning, gentlemen.

Froggatt   Morning, sir. You're in early this week.

Sir Richard   Know that. Have to get away sharpish, you see. My daughter's popping by to pick me up. Have her wait here for me, won't you? Clean towel in the loo?

Froggatt   I'll go and check, sir.

Sir Richard   Not been a phone call for me, has there?

Froggatt   Governor of the Bank of England. But he didn't leave a message.

Sir Richard   That's all right then. Deputy Chairman in? The Chief Executive?

Froggatt   None of the partners has arrived yet, sir.

Sir Richard   My God. I don't know what modern banking's coming to. There's a pondful of sharks out there. And some people seem to think we're still in an age when you could come wandering in at ten in the morning. What's the time now?

Froggatt   Ten in the morning, sir.

Wickerman   Good day, Sir Richard. How are we today?

Sir Richard   Quite nicely. What about you?

Wickerman   Not bad. I wonder if you'd just sign this?

Sir Richard *looks at him cunningly.*

Sir Richard   Aha, depends, doesn't it? What is it?

Wickerman   An authorization on this Kubinski business.

Sir Richard   Ah, Kubinski business, eh? Brief me, would you? The Kubinski business.

Wickerman   You mentioned it to me in confidence only last week.

Sir Richard   Only last week, did I really?

Wickerman   But I expect you'd had inside information.

Sir Richard   That's how it works, eh? Always keep three steps ahead of the game.

Wickerman   Quite right, Sir Richard. Just here.

Sir Richard *signs the document.*

Wickerman   Very good, sir. I'll get that processed at once.

Sir Richard   Good man. Always do good paperwork back-up, eh? That's always been the way at Battenberg's. You, what's your name?

Froggatt   I'm Froggatt, sir.

Sir Richard   Send the partners straight in to me, eh? Just as soon as they discover the energy to get here.

Sir Richard *goes into the Chairman's office.*

Froggatt   Oh, my God, what have you done now?

Wickerman   How do you mean?

Froggatt   What's that piece of paper?

Wickerman   Just a share purchase agreement I found in your drawer. Always do good paperwork back-up, eh?

Froggatt   You know what you are, Wickers? A bloody little swindler.

Wickerman   I'm sure we both have the best interests of the bank at heart. Oh, look. Tugs the heart-strings, doesn't it? You'd better let poor old Bennett in.

The **Beadle** *in the corridor, carrying with great difficulty, a large computer.* **Froggatt** *lets him in. Meanwhile* **Wickerman** *picks up the telephone and taps in some numbers.*

Beadle   Brought this up for you, sir. Desk's on its way.

Wickerman   Good work, Bennett. Don't try carrying the desk yourself, will you? We wouldn't want you to overdo it.

Beadle   Very thoughtful, Mr Wickerman. Thank you, sir.

The **Beadle** *goes.* **Wickerman** *on the phone.*

Wickerman (*phone*)   Oh, good morning, office of the Deputy Prime Minister? I'd like to speak to the Minister's Permanent Private Secretary . . . Oh, sorry, yes. This is Mr Tim Wickerman. Personal assistant to Sir Richard Battenberg at Battenberg's Bank . . .

Froggatt   What do you think you're up to now, Wickers?

Wickerman (*phone*)   Morning. Tim Wickerman, Battenberg's Bank. I wonder if you'd mind giving the Deputy Prime Minister a message? Yes, I'm sure Mr Heseltine is very busy. Sleaze does take up so much time, doesn't it? But it is rather urgent. In fact nasty questions in the House stuff, I'm afraid. I thought you'd expect us to warn you before the press pack got their teeth into it.

Froggatt   Got their teeth into what?

Wickerman It. Ssshhh . . . (*Phone*.) Perhaps Mr Heseltine could call Sir Richard back just as soon as he's out of Cabinet? It's about the Kubinski affair . . . Yes, of course. K . . . U . . . B . . . I . . . N. And then ski, as in his winter holiday . . . I'd rather not say any more now, it's extremely sensitive. And we don't want to end up with another BCCI scandal on our hands, do we? . . . Well, I'll try and detain him as long as I can, but Sir Richard does have another appointment in his diary soonest . . . Yes, I'll hold.

He puts his hand over the phone.

Wickerman Frog, just look up the number of the Department of Trade and Industry . . .

Froggatt What on earth has the bank got to do with Trade and Industry?

Wickerman And by the same token, what has trade and industry to do with this bank?

Back on the phone.

Oh yes, Mr Heseltine. Thank you for leaving the Cabinet, but it is rather urgent. Let me put you through to Sir Richard right away. (*Puts hand over the phone.*) How do I put him through to Sir Richard right away?

Froggatt *furiously comes to his desk telephone and presses a button.*

Wickerman You're through, Mr Heseltine. No no, this is his personal assistant. Tim Wickerman. Wickerman.

Wickerman *puts down the phone and smiles at* **Froggatt**. *Who is distraught.*

Froggatt And what do you think you've done now?

Wickerman I've arranged a telephone conference between Sir Richard and Michael Heseltine.

Froggatt About the Kubinski affair. And neither of them knows a rotten thing about the Kubinski affair.

Wickerman Not yet. But I'm sure they'll agree that if it requires all this high-level attention it must be pretty damned important.

Froggatt And what happens when both of them realize that neither of them knows a thing about it?

Wickerman In that case they'll have to turn to an expert who does know something about it.

Froggatt Nobody knows anything about it.

The lift pings.

Wickerman That's where you're wrong, Froggie. Fella at the door. See to it, would you?

Hartley Fenton, *CEO of Battenberg's Bank, a type with a smart striped shirt and a pinstriped suit, is being let in by the* **Beadle**. **Froggatt** *goes over to him.*

Froggatt Morning, Mr Fenton.

Fenton Chairman here already? Must have got up very early this morning?

Fenton *heads for the Chairman's office.* **Wickerman** *looks up.*

Wickerman Sorry, sir. Where do you think you're going?

Fenton Where am I going? I happen to be the Chief Executive Officer of this bank. And I have a meeting with my Chairman to discuss our profits and the corporate bottom line. Now, is that quite all right?

Wickerman I'm afraid you'll have to wait just a moment, sir. He's on the phone with the Deputy PM. If you'd just take a seat for a few seconds. Would you care for a coffee?

Fenton *unwillingly sits on the sofa.*

Fenton Very well.

Wickerman Black, white? Sugar, alternative additives?

Fenton Black with nothing.

Wickerman Froggatt, would you get the Chief Executive a black cup of coffee? Oh, and while you're there, could you ask my secretary to find me the Kubinski file?

Fenton Now look here, just who the hell are you?

Wickerman Who am I, Mr . . . ?

Fenton Fenton. Yes, just who the hell are you?

Wickerman *looks pained.*

Wickerman I'm the personal secretary to Sir Richard.

Fenton *looks at him mystified.*

Fenton I thought Froggatt was the personal secretary to Sir Richard.

Wickerman Yes, but the Chairman's workload has increased very considerably over the last day or so.

Fenton I know, Wimbledon fortnight is very demanding, isn't it?

Wickerman No, it's this, er, Kubinski affair.

Fenton This what?

Wickerman You've not been kept informed, then?

Fenton No, I haven't.

Wickerman Then I can only assume there's a strategic reason.

Sir Richard *appears from his office.*

Sir Richard You, young man. You're Wickerman, are you?

Wickerman Yes, course I am, sir.

Sir Richard The Deputy Prime Minister's asking for you. Wants a word about this Kurbachovsky affair.

Wickerman He's got it wrong, he must mean the Kubinski affair.

Sir Richard Anyway that's the joey.

Wickerman *picks up the phone.*

Wickerman (*phone*)   Tim Wickerman . . . Oh, good morning, Minister, how was Cabinet? . . . Good . . .

Sir Richard   Oh, there you are at last, Fenton. Been waiting, where were you?

Fenton   I was told to wait here for you, sir.

Wickerman (*phone*)   Oh dear, not had a proper briefing? It sounds as if the problem has to lie in your office, Minister. For some unexplained reason your officials haven't chosen to show you the files . . .

Sir Richard   Bloody government, typical.

Wickerman (*phone*)   Yes, I know . . . I know . . . Well, personally, I can't imagine why they'd choose to keep it from you. But you're certainly not to blame . . . If you like I'll come over to your office tomorrow and tell you how the thing looks to us from this end . . . Red tape, I know, I know . . . Yes, Minister.

Sir Richard   Sounds as if the problem's all at their end.

Wickerman   Rather looks like it, Sir Richard. But as you heard I lobbed the ball straight back into their court.

Sir Richard   Excellent work, Wickerman.

Wickerman   Oh, thank you, sir.

Sir Richard *is staring at him.*

Sir Richard   By the way, didn't I see you at Covent Garden the other night?

Wickerman   Actually I rather think it was Glyndebourne.

Sir Richard   Got you now. That's it, Glyndebourne. That was the night our picnic hamper was pinched.

Wickerman   Oh, dear, sir, was it really?

Sir Richard Didn't realize you actually worked here. Anyway you seem remarkably well abreast of this Krushchev affair.

Wickerman Kubinski affair. Well, I have been working day and night on it for weeks.

Fenton Nobody told me.

Sir Richard Maybe he should take charge of the whole thing. Eh, Fenton? I've got a pretty full plate as it is.

Fenton Well, it is Wimbledon. Look, sir, we seem to have a nasty problem blowing up with our Pacific Rim operations. Rogue trader. Do you mind if we have an urgent word?

The lift pings. **Helga Battenberg**, *the pretty young daughter of* **Sir Richard**, *very well and modernly dressed, appears beyond the glass door and waves for attention.*

Sir Richard There's my daughter come to fetch me. Let her in, Wickerman. Nothing serious, is it?

Helga *comes over and kisses* **Sir Richard**.

Fenton Our man in Hong Kong has been gambling the Chinese would refuse to take back the colony . . .

Sir Richard What man in Hong Kong?

Helga About ready, Pop?

Fenton Our office there. It does half the bank's trading. This was the chap who lost us thirty million because he had inside news Gorbachev was going to be re-elected in Russia.

Sir Richard Bloody fool. Where is he?

Fenton We don't know. But Interpol are looking for him now.

Sir Richard Look, you'd better come in for a minute. Wickerman, would you mind just entertaining my daughter?

Sir Richard *and* **Fenton** *go into the Chairman's office.* **Helga** *sits on the sofa and looks at* **Wickerman**.

Helga Very well, go on. Do what the man says.

Wickerman   I'll start with a song entitled . . .

Helga (*stares at him*)   Hold it. Just a minute. Don't I know you from somewhere?

Wickerman   Well, we have met several times. Hither and thither. Across a crowded lawn.

Helga   Like where?

Wickerman   Like last week at Glyndebourne for instance?

Helga   Oh God, yes. What was that god-awful opera we saw that night?

Wickerman   *The Marriage of Figaro*? Actually I didn't see it that night. I gave my ticket to a friend. And spent the evening having a long but lovely picnic.

Helga   Well, you didn't miss much. It was all classical music from beginning to end. I bet the old git works you pretty hard, doesn't he?

Wickerman   The old git? Oh, you mean your father. Yes, at the moment. But then we're right up to our nosebags in it over this Kubinski business. Fantastic project. He's probably told you.

Helga   I bet. Do you really like working in the bank? Just wheeling and dealing and trading and raiding and buying and selling?

Wickerman   The way the British economy's functioning at the moment, I like working. Period.

Helga   I think it's boring. And you do know what he pays, don't you? Well, of course, you do, because he pays you. Not very well, I bet.

Wickerman   I can certainly say my wages aren't anything like commensurate with the amount of work I'm doing.

Helga   That's because he's the classic feudal capitalist. And you know what they do, don't you?

Wickerman Exploit the proletariat, you mean? And grind the faces of the economically disadvantaged?

Helga I don't know about that. But they manipulate the entire world economy through loaded fiscal transactions. Leading to deprivation in the Third World, and the depletion of the natural eco-system of our nurturing mother planet.

Wickerman I see you went to the University of Essex.

Helga (*interested in him*) No, I didn't. It was Sussex. What's your name?

Wickerman I'm Tim. Tim Wickerman.

Helga Like real music, Tim?

Wickerman What do you mean by real music?

Helga Anything that's not *Marriage of Figaro*.

Wickerman Yeah, I love it.

Helga Me too. Know any places?

Wickerman Yeah, I know all the places. Want me to take you?

Helga What, tonight? Oh shag it, I can't. We've got a dinner party. I mean, a dinner party! With all the BOFS.

Wickerman BOFS?

Helga Boring Old Farts. Oh, there you are, Pop.

Sir Richard *and* **Fenton** *reappear.*

Fenton Maybe you should fly out there right away and investigate.

Sir Richard Hong Kong? Love to. Trouble is I'm totally tied up with this Korbachovsky business. Why don't you send one of the other partners? If they ever choose to arrive.

Helga Pop, I've just had a really whizz idea. Why not invite Tim to your dinner party tonight?

Sir Richard Tim?

Wickerman   I'm Tim.

Sir Richard   But isn't Stephen coming?

Helga   No, he's going to the opera. Meaning I won't have anyone to talk to.

Sir Richard   All right then, Tim. I'll send the Bentley over about seven. And in the meantime I leave things in your very capable hands.

Froggatt *appears with a cup of coffee.*

Froggatt   There we are, sir. It's instant, I'm afraid.

Fenton   Except it wasn't, Froggatt, was it? I'm beginning to wonder about you.

At the door, **Wickerman** *makes a fuss of* **Sir Richard**.

Wickerman   Thank you, Sir Richard. Oh, there is one thing. I did wonder, well . . .

Sir Richard   Go on, man, what is it?

Wickerman   Don't really like to ask, sir. But it's this huge workload I'm landed with over the Kubinski business . . . I just wondered if I could have Mr Froggatt as my personal assistant?

Froggatt *nearly drops the coffee.*

Froggatt   You, you . . .

Sir Richard   Think you can work well together, do you?

Wickerman   I have had Froggatt under me before, sir.

Sir Richard   Seems a top flight idea. Consider it done. And see you round seven thirty then, Tim.

Wickerman   Looking forward to it. Bye then, Helga.

Helga   Cheers, Tim.

Helga *and* **Sir Richard** *go*.

Froggatt   Now I'm working under you?

Wickerman   We've always been a team, haven't we, Frog?

Froggatt No, we haven't. And I've been demoted.

Wickerman On the other hand, I've been promoted.

Froggatt And now you're after the boss's daughter.

Wickerman It's what we Fuggers always do.

Froggatt Well, you're making a big mistake. She's engaged to Stephen Fabry. Who may be a world-class prat, but he's not a total shit like you. And he's got real money. And he's not unemployed.

Wickerman Take it easy, Frog, you're overwrought. If not old-fashioned.

Froggatt Anyone who met you would be over . . .

The lift pings. **Paston-Jones,** *the Deputy Chairman, comes in. A stout man in country-style clothes, he's the sort of man who would look better on the back of a hunter.*

Paston-Jones Morning, gents. Sorry I'm late. Been to the health farm for a Dyna-rod.

Froggatt Oh, good morning, Mr Paston-Jones.

Paston-Jones Met Sir Richard as I was unwrapping myself from the lift. He's already filled me in. Seems devilish caught up with this Kubinski business.

Wickerman Is he really, sir?

Paston-Jones Wanted to know when we last discussed it fully at board level. Told him I really don't think we ever did.

Wickerman You must have done, sir. Sorry, I'm Tim Wickerman. Sir Richard's personal assistant.

Paston-Jones *looks at* **Froggatt.**

Paston-Jones I thought he was Dickie's PA.

Wickerman No, I'm Dickie's PA. And he's my PA.

Paston-Jones Never mind, Lord Holbeck will fill us in. He'll remember. He's got a memory like an elephant. Damn well looks like one too.

The lift pings. **Lord Holbeck**, *an elderly squirearchical gent of the Harold Macmillan breed, stands in the doorway.*

Lord Holbeck   What will I remember?

Paston-Jones   Ah, Lord Holbeck. How's the farming?

Lord Holbeck   Like a bloody Great War battlefield. Dead cows all over the place. Farmin's not what it was. We used to have decent diseases. What was wrong with Foot and Mouth? Eh, what will I remember?

Fenton   Do you remember something called the Kubinski affair?

Lord Holbeck *parks himself on the sofa.*

Lord Holbeck   Do I remember? Course I do.

Paston-Jones   You actually remember it?

Lord Holbeck   Yes. I remember it.

Paston-Jones   What?

Lord Holbeck   Quite a time back, of course. Duggie-Home was PM at the time, I recall. Nice man, you know. Deserved better.

Fenton   The Kubinski affair, Lord Holbeck.

Lord Holbeck   It was property boom. Kubinski was a developer. Had this amazing new method for building high-rise blocks for city councils and private clients. Bloody awful things. Hamster cages in the sky, I called them.

Fenton   Well?

Lord Holbeck   Worked up a great scheme for building hundreds of these damned things on Greenwich Marshes. Only problem was the flats were tall and the marshes were wet. They are, you know. Two winters later half the buildings ended up three storeys shorter than they started. Lost half a dozen tenants with them too.

Paston-Jones   Wasn't there a scandal?

Lord Holbeck   Course there was a scandal. It was scandalous, you see. They blamed the Minister, half a dozen local councillors, the architect, the contractor, the surveyor. And old Peter Kubinski, of course. That's why they called it the Kubinski affair.

Fenton   Surely there was an enquiry?

Lord Holbeck   Naturally there was an enquiry, there's always an enquiry.

Fenton   Well, what did it find out?

Lord Holbeck   What did it find out? What do enquiries find out? Unfortunate decisions taken. Insufficient consultation. Inattention to detail. No single individual to blame.

Paston-Jones   And was the bank involved?

Lord Holbeck   Course the bank was involved. The bank put up the money. Hell of a lot of it. Naturally it disappeared down the thunderbox when Kubinski stopped trading. And we ended up with dead and useless stock.

Fenton   So why has it all surfaced again?

Lord Holbeck   I dunno. Thought it was all decently dead and buried. We paid enough in lawyers' fees.

Paston-Jones   Do you know why, Wickerman?

Wickerman   Maybe it's something to do with Jurgen Fabry. I heard they'd been showing interest in the company. And of course now the Deputy Prime Minister has got involved . . .

Lord Holbeck *stares at* **Wickerman**.

Lord Holbeck   Who the devil are you?

Wickerman   Sorry, sir?

Fenton   Oh, that's Wickerman, Lord Holbeck.

Lord Holbeck   New, are you?

Wickerman   Oh no, sir.

Paston-Jones   Been with the bank for many years.

Lord Holbeck   Never seen him before. And I know practically everyone at Battenberg's. What department?

Wickerman   Futures and Options. Ventures. Risks.

Lord Holbeck   I used to be in charge of Futures. Been here for years? Get away with you, young man.

Fenton   Come now, Lord Holbeck. We can't always remember everything. Let's go into the Chairman's office and discuss this properly.

They all go toward the Chairman's office. **Lord Holbeck** *turns.*

Lord Holbeck   I remember everything. And I bloody don't remember you.

They go in.

Wickerman   Well, at least now we know. What the Kubinski business is.

Froggatt   And now Lord Holbeck knows you're a fraud.

Wickerman   But the others think he's lost his marbles.

Froggatt   They'd believe him if I said so too.

Wickerman   But you wouldn't, would you, Frog?

Froggatt   Why wouldn't I? You've just sodding well robbed me of my job, Wickers.

Wickerman *advances on* **Froggatt**.

Wickerman   Because you wouldn't, you little oink.

Froggatt *is pushed down over the desk,* **Wickerman** *over him, pinning him down.*

Froggatt   Get off me, Wickers, you greasy beast.

Wickerman   You know what we do with turdy little sneaks, don't you?

Fenton, **Paston-Jones** *and* **Holbeck** *come out of the office.*

Fenton   Let me have bankers about me who are hungry, that's what I always say. Anything wrong, Wickerman?

The executives stand and stare. **Wickerman** *lets the wriggling* **Froggatt** *go.*

Wickerman   Sorry, sir. Just checking Froggatt's back teeth. He was complaining of a little dental trouble. You'll be fine, Froggie. Just don't forget to floss. Oh, Mr Fenton, I wondered if you'd reached any conclusions on the Kubinski affair?

Fenton   We've thought we'd potter over to White's. And discuss it in depth over eel pie and claret.

They head for the exit. **Wickerman** *coughs loudly.*

Wickerman   Mr Fenton. I think I heard you say you liked bankers who were hungry?

Fenton *turns and looks at him.*

Fenton   Quite. Oh look, yes, why don't you join us? You seem to be the only one in the building who really knows anything about this business . . .

Wickerman   It does look like that. Always happy to assist. Hats and coats, Froggatt.

Fenton   Just as long as the Chairman's office is properly covered over lunch-time trading.

Wickerman   No problem there. Now I've got my own assistant. Look, Froggatt, if anyone calls, could you tell them I'm out lunching with the CEO? At our club?

All go except **Froggatt**. *Who sits at his desk, puts his head in his hands.*

Froggatt   Bastard. Filthy oinkish bastard.

Maybelle *comes from her office.*

Maybelle   I'm just off for lunch at Pastrami Heaven. Can I bring you back a BLT?

Froggatt   Yes, all right, then.

Maybelle   Mayonnaise?

Froggatt   Make it rat poison.

Maybelle   Whatever suits your lifestyle, Mr Froggatt.

Maybelle *goes. The phone rings.* **Froggatt** *picks it up.*

Froggatt (*phone*)   Oh, yes, Governor. No, the Chairman's out to lunch . . . The Vice-Chairman's out to lunch . . . The Chief Executive? Out to lunch . . . Sir Richard's personal assistant? He's definitely out to lunch, over at White's . . . No one's here. Except me, of course. I'm here, I'm always here . . . Me, I'm personal assistant to the personal assistant . . . It's like the third first assistant director on a film . . . No, I do realize you can't deal with small fry. I'll get one of the bigger fry to ring you. When they get back, probably around four . . . Yes, Governor. Thank you for calling Battenberg's. Where your security is our confidence . . .

Froggatt *puts down the phone.*

Act Two

A week later.

*Same set reordered: the boardroom at Battenberg's. As the set is not naturalistic, the same background of corridor and rooms off is retained. But the desk centre stage has been replaced with a large conference table. A four-cornered Battenberg logo hangs clearly on the wall. Preparations for a major board meeting. **Maybelle** is putting out notepads on the table. The **Beadle** is setting up an overhead projector and screen – which needs to be functioning for later.*

The phone on the side-table rings. **Maybelle** *answers.*

Maybelle (*phone*)   Conference room, Battenberg's Bank . . . Mr Wickerman? No, sorry. He's over at the Bank of England, with the Governor . . . No, his personal organizer is very full today. He's got an extraordinary board meeting as soon as he gets back . . . Yes, I should, Monsieur Chirac. Try him tomorrow or the next day. Thank you for calling Battenberg's. Where your security is our confidence.

Beadle   You know, it's funny, isn't it? I still remember the day Mr Timothy first joined the bank. Ten, twelve years back it'd got to be . . .

Maybelle   He must have come here straight from school then.

Beadle   Bushy-tailed and bright-eyed, he was. You could tell he was going to be one of the high-flyers even then.

Maybelle   You do know how to spot them, Mr Bennett.

Beadle   Mrs Thatcher time it was. That was the big boom. Just before the great crash. He never turned his eyes away from those dealing screens. If rubbers were up or coppers were dropping, first one to spot it was always young Mr Timothy. Always into strings and straddles. You could tell he wasn't like all the other traders.

Maybelle   Didn't come from Essex for one thing, did he?

Beadle   Highly educated man, Mr Timothy. Civil. A
levels. Knows how to treat you, know what I mean?
Unlike . . .

The **Beadle** *nods knowingly as* **Froggatt** *comes in, still taking off
his cycling gear.*

Froggatt   What's going on here then?

Maybelle   Extraordinary board meeting, Mr Froggatt.

Froggatt *puts his bicycle wheel in the cupboard.*

Froggatt   Don't tell me. Let me guess. Mr Wickerman.

Beadle   . . . Has called a special meeting.

Froggatt   About the Kubinski affair.

Maybelle   How did you know that?

Froggatt   Because, my dear Maybelle, I've about had it up
to here with the Kubinski affair. We've heard about nothing
else in this bloody bank for the whole of the last week. All
other business has ceased. Letters and faxes aren't being
answered. Nobody does the accounts and settlements. There
could be a bloody world war going on out there . . .

Maybelle   Is there?

Froggatt   I don't know, I listen to local radio. But there
could be, and nobody in this bank would notice, because
they're all devoting all their attention to . . .

Maybelle   The Kubinski affair.

Froggatt   Exactly.

Maybelle   You're not saying it's only a storm in a teacup?

Froggatt   I'm saying it's not even a real teacup. Here,
what do you want?

The lift pings. The **Old Man** *from Act One appears again.*

Old Man   I wondered if I could see the Chairman and the
partners.

Froggatt   What, to shine their shoes?

Old Man   My personal valeting service, sir. I do the Chairman and partners in most of the other banks. I'm sure Battenberg's wouldn't want to be left behind. I thought if I could just have a few words with the Chairman . . .

Froggatt   If you want a few words with the Chairman, here's what you do. You call the switchboard and ask for the personal assistant to the company secretary. If she thinks you deserve an appointment, she'll call the assistant to the Chief Executive's secretary.

Maybelle   If she thinks it's important, she'll ring the Chairman's secretary. Who happens to be me . . .

Froggatt   And if she thinks it's important, she'll tell the Chairman's personal assistant's personal assistant, which is me. If I think it's relevant I'll then tell Mr Wickerman . . .

Maybelle   But unfortunately Mr Wickerman is so busy at the moment he couldn't possibly have any time to deal with it.

Froggatt   So now you've saved yourself a whole lot of telephoning, I think the best thing you can do is just sod off, don't you?

Old Man   I really would like a brief word with the Chairman. Can't you just take my name?

Froggatt   No, I can't take your name, because we're just about to begin a very important board meeting. Bennett, would you escort this gentleman out of here?

Beadle   Come on, sir. You heard what the man said.

Maybelle   And thank you for thinking of Battenberg's Bank.

The **Beadle** *escorts the* **Old Man** *from the room.*

Maybelle   You strike me as on a bit of a short fuse today, Mr Froggatt.

Froggatt   Short fuse? Why would I be on a short fuse?

Maybelle   Could it be the snooker?

Froggatt   That spotty oink Stephen Hendry did win again.
But no, Maybelle, it's not snooker that shortens my fuse.

Maybelle   You're not getting a little bit jealous of Mr
Wickerman?

Froggatt   Aren't I? Miss Dodds, a week ago I was an up
and coming banking executive, wasn't I? A fast-track
recruit. A headhunter's dream.

Maybelle   True enough.

Froggatt   No one in this bank was upper or more coming
than I was. I worked hard for years, right? When all my
friends were taking their little pills down the disco, I was
doing algebra and alogarithims, wasn't I? I went to the poly
and took courses in macro-economics and creative
accountancy. Commercial law and fund management.
Futures and derivatives. Computing skills and managerial
efficiency. I trained my mind. I worked on my body, turned
it into the lean mean machine it is today. I was first in here
every morning, last out every night. I didn't eat lunch, I had
carrots for dinner. Then what happens?

Maybelle   Some little smartarse from nowhere walks in off
the street and takes your job. He gets in minutes what you've
been after for years.

Froggatt   I'm glad somebody noticed, Maybelle.

Maybelle   It's obvious. And he wouldn't even have got his
foot in the door if it hadn't been for your good nature. Now
he's upgrading your old job, and you're just his henchman.
You stay in watching snooker, he's dating the boss's
daughter. He's driving a company Porsche, you're driving a
company Skoda.

Froggatt   Company bike, actually.

Maybelle   Anyway it's only human to be jealous.

Froggatt   What makes you think I'm jealous?

Maybelle   Course you are. You have every right.

Froggatt   Good. Thank you. I'm jealous.

Maybelle   But what you should do is look at it creatively. See it as a great self-empowerment opportunity.

Froggatt   You've been talking to your aromatherapist again, haven't you, Maybelle?

Maybelle *comes close.*

Maybelle   How did you know I had aromatherapy?

Froggatt   I have a nose for these things. What do you mean, self-empowerment opportunity?

Maybelle   Mr Wickerman's a natural high-flyer, right?

Froggatt   A big swinging dick, yes.

Maybelle   He's bound to reach the top echelons, isn't he? Board material.

Froggatt   Only if nobody catches him first.

Maybelle   If you were to hitch your wagon to his star . . .

Froggatt   I've no intention of hitching my wagon to Mr Oink Wickerman's clapped out little star. Mr Wickerman can just stick his little star . . .

Maybelle   Morning, Mr Wickerman.

Wickerman *has come in, in a fine new suit. He seems just a little anxious.*

Wickerman   Morning to you, Maybelle. Everything ready for the Kubinski presentation?

Maybelle   Yes, Mr Wickerman. Overhead projector, slides and transparencies . . .

Wickerman   Let's just check the list of people attending.

Maybelle   Right, Mr Wickerman. Chairman, Deputy Chairman, Chief Executive, Senior Partner. Lord Fabry from Jurgen Fabry. Mr Fitzroy, the Junior Minister from the Deputy Prime Minister's office.

Froggatt   Oh yes? Really, the Junior Minister?

Maybelle   So would you like me to get those transparencies ready now?

Wickerman   You do that, Maybelle. Good stuff.

Maybelle *goes into her office.* **Wickerman** *turns to* **Froggatt**.

Wickerman   What's the matter with you, Froggie? You seem to have cheered up all of a sudden.

Froggatt   Oh, do I?

Wickerman   What is it, Frog?

Froggatt   The truth is I just can't wait, Wickers. Half the biggest players in the Square Mile are going to park their backsides in our little boardroom. Only to find they're wasting their working time discussing a non-existent company. And the fraudulent dealings of a bank employee who for some reason isn't even on the payroll. And you haven't really prepared a thing, have you?

Wickerman   Things have snowballed a bit, I have to admit.

Froggatt   Well, don't count on me. Because what I'm going to do now is trot over to the Old Bailey and book front row seats for the fraud Trial of the Century. Eat your heart out, Kevin Maxwell.

Wickerman   Now now, Froggie, we're old friends, remember. We're both in this one together.

Froggatt   No, we're not, Wickers. We're not old friends. And one thing we're definitely not in is this one together.

Sir Richard *comes in from the corridor.*

Sir Richard   Ah, morning there, Tim. Morning, er . . .

Froggatt   Froggatt, Sir Richard.

Sir Richard *looks round, takes* **Wickerman** *by the arm and leads him stage front.*

Sir Richard   Look, old boy, quiet word, man to man. I need to feel abreast.

Wickerman   You need to feel a breast, sir?

Sir Richard   I appear to be going naked into the conference chamber. I don't seem to have been provided with any briefs at all. Hence I need to feel abreast.

Wickerman   Are you all right, Sir Richard? Oh, you're talking about this Kubinski business.

Sir Richard   Isn't that what I said?

Wickerman   Sir Richard, to tell the truth I've had to set this meeting up with very little preparation. Because we suddenly got all this Government interest. Thanks to your very useful talk with Mr Heseltine. I just don't know how you do it.

Sir Richard   Yes, went well, didn't it? Trouble is, we have all this top brass coming. And for the life of me I can't exactly remember the bank's grand and historic role in this Klempinksi affair.

Wickerman   What is it you need to remember exactly?

Sir Richard   Well, roughly speaking, what it's about.

Wickerman   What about what it's about?

Sir Richard   I want to know when the shenanigans actually started. How Battenberg's got involved. What our commitment is. How much we're in for. So if you'd quickly dig out the original paperwork . . .

Wickerman   The original *paper*work, sir?

Sir Richard   Yes, for ten generations we've always worked on paper in this bank. If I've insisted on anything in my time here, it's that we always keep paper back-up.

Wickerman   Really?

Sir Richard   Tradition, you see. My great-great-grandfather worked on paper. My great-grandfather worked on paper. My grand . . .

Wickerman   Yes, sir, I think I've got the point. Mr Froggatt. Would you go down to the filing room and bring me all the original papers on the Kubinski affair?

Froggatt   You want me to go to records and dig out all the original paper on . . .

Wickerman   The Kubinski affair. Right now, Froggatt. The meeting begins in fifteen minutes.

Froggatt   And if there isn't any paper on the Kubinski affair?

Wickerman *hurries him toward the door.*

Wickerman   If there's a filing room, there's bound to be paper. Find something and bring it here.

Sir Richard   Problem, Tim?

Wickerman   Just briefing Froggatt on what to look for.

Froggatt *goes, in some delight.* **Wickerman** *returns to* **Sir Richard***, who is seated at the table, mopping his brow.*

Wickerman   Are you really all right, sir?

Sir Richard   Course. Truth is, Tim, I'm getting in a real sweat over this Korbachevsky business. I've never been a hands-on chairman. Others may be, but that's not been my way. If you appoint top quality staff, there's no reason why they shouldn't be left to get on with the job.

Wickerman   While you go out hunting with the Cottesmore?

Sir Richard   Exactly. That's always been my method. That is how I see it. You see the results.

Wickerman   Quite.

Sir Richard   You're sure there's nothing to worry about? You couldn't have overlooked something? Pushed things through a little bit too hurriedly? Failed to exercise due discretion?

Wickerman   It's always been my method, Sir Richard.
Get in three steps ahead of the competition. Bite the ass off
the bear, eh? Remember, he who dares wins.

Sir Richard   Yes, well, of course. That's why we pay out a
fortune for top-flight players like you. Came a bit of a
cropper with this chap in Hong Kong though, I can tell you.

Wickerman   They haven't found him yet?

Sir Richard   No. Police are hopeless. The only people who
seem to have any hint of his whereabouts are Diners Club.
But that's the trouble now. A lot of the people we deal with in
banking these days are well, quite frankly, not . . .

Wickerman   Not . . . ?

Sir Richard   No. Some of them are very un . . .

Wickerman   Sorry to hear it, sir.

Sir Richard   It's the way the world wags, now. Banking
used to be an honourable business.

Wickerman   It certainly did.

Sir Richard   Look at Rothschild, won the battle of
Waterloo with a pigeon. Think of the great names. Barclay
and Gurney. Gresham and Baring. Schroeder and Warburg.
Morgan and Frick. Good men, Wickerman. Sat on the back
of fifteen hands of horseflesh like a Christian. Men who built
the empire. Jardine and Matthison. Railways in India.
Mines in Africa. Opium in China. Founders of nations,
Wickerman. Salt of the earth.

Wickerman   Absolutely, sir.

Sir Richard   Then look at banking now. Lads with a
mobile phone in one ear and a Walkman in the other selling
futures as if there was no tomorrow. It's not banking, it's
trading. I blame Madame Thatcher.

Wickerman   Quite.

Sir Richard   I remember the days when money used to be
money. Copper and silver and gold. You could bite the stuff,

Wickerman. Hide it under your bed. Smuggle it into
Liechtenstein at the drop of a socialist hat. Now what is it?
Flickers on a silver screen. One minute you're staring at an
investment of ten million yen, the next it's Cilla Black doing
Blind Date. You see, there's no reality in cash and coin any
more. No real people in banking either. Not like those men
up there.

He gestures to the portraits on the walls.

Wickerman   Don't upset yourself, Sir Richard. I honestly
don't think the other side have put nearly as much research
into the Kubinski affair as we have.

Sir Richard   How much do you reckon they know?

Wickerman   It's more a question of what they don't
know. My guess is once you get them round the table you'll
find they know nothing at all.

Sir Richard *checks his watch.*

Sir Richard   Where the devil's Froggatt? Look, we'd
better just go into my suite and get me abreast . . .

*They disappear into the Chairman's office. The **Beadle** comes in from
the corridor with **Paston-Jones** and **Lord Holbeck**. These two
sit down at the conference table.*

Paston-Jones   Damn ridiculous. We should have had
papers.

Beadle   I understand Mr Wickerman had to organize this
meeting in rather a hurry.

Paston-Jones   Wickerman, Wickerman. It's always
Wickerman these days, isn't it?

Lord Holbeck   Remember him, you know.

Paston-Jones   What?

Lord Holbeck   To think that twenty years ago when I
worked here he was only a junior clerk.

Paston-Jones   That would make him remarkably young,
wouldn't it?

Lord Holbeck   Sat in my office. Next to the window.

Paston-Jones   Are you sure, Lord Holbeck?

Lord Holbeck   As true as I'm holding this glass.

Which he isn't. **Fenton** *comes bustling in, looks round.*

Fenton   Sir Richard not here yet?

Paston-Jones   I think he's debriefing in his office.

Fenton *sits down conspiratorially.*

Fenton   Good. Because I've something to say to you both.
Before this meeting starts. On the q.t. Strictly between
ourselves. I've been thinking about the bottom line on this
Kubinski business. I wondered whether it's occurred to you,
as it has to me, that we've all been thoroughly taken for a
ride?

Paston-Jones   Go on, Fenton. I've been wondering
myself.

Fenton   Well, I can only say in all my wide executive
experience I've never seen a board meeting arranged like
this. No papers, no back-up. No prior information, no
agenda.

Lord Holbeck   I remember there was an occasion once in
Wigan. That was when Duggie-Home was still PM . . .

Fenton   Yes, Lord Holbeck. The truth is we've come to this
meeting with a pistol held against our heads, right? I don't
like to name names . . .

They all lean in closer.

Paston-Jones   But you're talking about Wickerman.

Fenton   Let me be the first to express my admiration for
Wickerman. You saw the other day I took him to White's.
Not a thing a man does lightly. I realize he's a close friend of
the Chairman . . .

Paston-Jones   And of his daughter.

Fenton　But when it comes to banking, everything has to be right out in the open.

Paston-Jones　Unless it's a question of extreme discretion. In which case it's totally confidential.

Lord Holbeck　Don't understand a bloody word you're talking about, Fenton. Never did.

Fenton　I'm pointing out this meeting is *ultra vires*, Lord Holbeck. Right off the wall. Improperly convened. By Mr Wickerman. And the big question is – why?

Lord Holbeck　Why?

Fenton　Because he doesn't, can't allow the real truth to come out.

Lord Holbeck　Which is?

Fenton (*leans in even closer*)　Which is that I was the one who initiated this whole Kubinski venture. As some of you will doubtless recall.

Lord Holbeck　I don't. I did most of the early preparation.

Paston-Jones　I worked out the original figures.

Lord Holbeck　I raised the matter in the Lords.

Fenton　Well, exactly. You see what I'm saying.

Lord Holbeck　You mean . . . ?

Fenton　Precisely.

Lord Holbeck　Precisely what?

Fenton　There's a huge deal brewing in the bank, right? And Wickerman's trying to shut us out.

Paston-Jones　That's why there are no papers, Lord Holbeck. And why there'll be no bonuses for us.

Lord Holbeck　Ah. Ah! But that's outrageous, isn't it? This is why there are no papers.

Fenton *puts his finger to his lips.* **Sir Richard** *and* **Wickerman** *have come from the Chairman's office. They take their seats at the table.*

Sir Richard   Morning, gentlemen. We seem to be fairly quorate. And we have our friends from Fabry and the Junior Minister joining us at eleven. So may I ask Mr Wickerman to open discussion on the . . .

Fenton   Point of order, Mr Chairman. May I say all those present are extremely unhappy about the conduct of this meeting?

Sir Richard   Unhappy at the conduct of . . . ?

Fenton   In fact we question whether it can properly take place at all.

Sir Richard   But it already is.

Fenton   We have no briefing papers, no figures, no mission statements, no agenda. All due respect to Wickerman, but in our view this entire matter has been completely mishandled.

Paston-Jones   Quite unlike the Kubinski venture in the past.

Fenton   We've all worked on Kubinski. We've sweated for Kubinski. And now Mr Wickerman seems determined to steal all the credit.

Wickerman   I assure you, gentlemen, if you'd rather steal all the credit . . .

Sir Richard   I hear what you're saying. In fact it occurred to me. Which is why I sent for the original papers. Where are they, Wickerman?

Wickerman   I sent Froggatt to get them.

Lord Holbeck   Oh, not Froggatt. Never did trust Froggatt to do anything.

Froggatt *comes in.*

Sir Richard   There you are, Froggatt. Well? Have you found those papers?

Froggatt   Well, no, sir.

Wickerman   No, Froggatt?

Froggatt   No, Mr Wickerman. Because there aren't any.

The board members look at each other, then at **Froggatt**.

Sir Richard   Froggatt. Are you seriously saying that
crucial banking documents can disappear completely? Just
half an hour before a major conference?

Froggatt   Yes, sir.

Wickerman   You did look properly, did you, Froggatt?

Froggatt   I looked absolutely everywhere. There's
nothing at all on Kubinski.

Paston-Jones   Of course there is. We all worked on it.

Wickerman   I do have to say I find this very hard to
believe, Sir Richard.

Sir Richard   I think we should adjourn for fifteen minutes.
Retire to my suite for a contemplative glass of sherry. Aye?

'Ayes' all round. The board members rise.

Lord Holbeck   In my day, a decent chap in Froggatt's
position would have gone out and shot himself.

Sir Richard   Perhaps nowadays we ought to try to look for
a more civilized solution. And meantime Mr Wickerman can
go and find the papers.

The board members go off to the Chairman's room. **Wickerman**
crosses to **Froggatt** *and grabs him.*

Wickerman   You bloody fool, Froggie. You could have
come up with something. Any old papers would have done.
What do we do now?

Froggatt   Look here, Wickers, do you mind not including
me in your plans any more? In fifteen minutes they're going
to skin you alive right here on this boardroom table. And I
really don't want any part in it.

Wickerman   You are part of it. Who recruited me into this
bank in the first place?

Froggatt   I never asked you to come into the bank. You pushed your way in. And ever since you've been trying to drive me out of it.

Wickerman   Come on, Frog. You're not going to betray the big dream, are you?

Froggatt   Big dream? What dream? Until ten minutes ago, I thought the worst that could happen was I'd end up on the street with you, selling *Big Issue*. Now it looks as if we'll end up in Ford open prison. Doing push-ups with half the rest of the City of London.

Wickerman   Think of the big dream, Frog. The dream of creating a multi-million pound business from a company that doesn't even exist. Just imagine.

Froggatt   Imagine what?

Wickerman (*exhilarated*)   A company that's no more than a flicker on the TV screen. A company that doesn't make anything. Doesn't employ anybody. Doesn't underpay its workers. Doesn't deplete anything. Doesn't pollute anything. A company that's eco-friendly. Its waste never goes into the rivers. It has no effect on the ozone layer. Its animal rights record is superb. Wouldn't you want to invest in a company like that, Frog?

Froggatt   You're talking about a bloody fraud, Wickerman.

Wickerman   No, I'm not. I'm talking about the perfect company. I'm talking about a . . . Platonic ideal, Froggie.

Froggatt   You always were a total crap artist, Wickers.

The lift pings. **Helga** *appears in the corridor and taps on the glass.*

Wickerman   Let her in, Frog. And then disappear, all right?

Froggatt *looks at him, goes to the door and lets* **Helga** *in, goes off.* **Helga** *comes in close.*

Helga   Sorry, Tim. I suppose this is a bad moment. But I remembered this is your really big day. So I thought I'd come in and wish you luck.

Wickerman   Luck?

Helga   This Kubinski venture. I mean, you have buzzed on about it every single night this week we've gone out together. I understand, Tim. I know what it means to you.

Wickerman *steps away from her*.

Wickerman   Very kind of you, Helga.

Helga *looks at him*.

Helga   Is everything all right? You've got this look . . .

Wickerman   No, Helga, everything isn't all right. In fact it's pretty well all wrong. You might as well know now. Before your father tells you. This Kubinski venture . . . well, the honest truth is, there is no Kubinski venture.

Helga   Of course there is. A truly modern company. Green, innovative. The government's going to invest in it. You told me all about it. Every night this week.

Wickerman   All right. I invented this dream company. The trouble is, Helga, it is a dream. A fiction. You know, a kind of illusion.

Helga   You mean it's a great and glorious vision?

Wickerman   Or another word would be scam.

Helga *stares at him*.

Helga   You mean you just made the whole thing up?

Wickerman   Yes. But think of it. A company that's just a piece of paper. A flash on a screen. It does this and it does that. One day its price goes down, another day it goes up. One day everybody buys, the next day everybody sells. One day it's surging in Tokyo, the next it's sinking in Frankfurt. One minute it's about to be taken over, the next it's executing a dawn raid. A company like that could keep millions of people happy.

Helga *looks at him.*

Helga Tim . . . I think that's great.

Wickerman I think it's great. The trouble is, the board of Battenberg's isn't going to agree with you.

Helga Why not?

Wickerman I suppose mostly because the scam's all being done with their capital.

Helga You mean it's a scam against the bank you're working for?

Wickerman Ah, well, that's another thing. Work for them, yes, but only in a very abstract sense. I mean, I'm not actually on the payroll or anything.

Helga I don't understand.

Wickerman Well, if Kubinski's a sort of dream company, I'm just a sort of dream employee.

Helga But you're the best in the bank. Pop says so. You mean he doesn't pay you?

Wickerman He probably thinks he pays me. But since I'm not actually on the payroll, I never see a single cent.

Helga That's terrible, Tim. I really think you should sue.

Wickerman Yes, but if they found out I wasn't really here in the first place, they might not want me here in the second place. If you see what I mean.

Helga Why didn't you tell me this before, Tim?

Wickerman Well, you are the Chairman's daughter. Anyway, I thought if anyone found out who I actually was, or in this case wasn't, they'd kick me out. And then I'd never see you again.

Helga And you really wanted to see me again?

Wickerman Of course I really wanted to see you again. You've got my stereo, for one thing. But I don't suppose I shall, because they're certain to kick me out anyway.

Helga   How are they going to find out?

Wickerman   They've asked me to find the back file on the Kubinski business. And the trouble is, there isn't one.

Helga   Yes there is.

Wickerman   No there isn't, because I made it up.

Helga *looks at him.*

Helga   Yes, there is. Leave it to me.

Sir Richard *emerges from his suite, anxiously looking at his watch.*

Sir Richard   Only five more minutes to go. Found those files yet, Wickerman?

Helga   Hello, Pop.

Sir Richard   Helga! What are you doing here? We're in the middle of an important meeting.

Helga   Sorry, Pop. But I just wanted to make sure it was all OK about those Kubinski files I gave you.

A beat.

Sir Richard   Kubinski files you gave me?

Helga   You haven't forgotten, have you, Dad?

Sir Richard   Course not. What?

Helga   It was a big fat dusty file. I handed it to you this morning when you were going out.

Sir Richard   Oh yes? And why would you have it?

Helga *glances round.*

Helga   Because Tim brought it over to the house last week for safe-keeping. And he told me to make quite sure you had it today. You have checked out your briefcase this morning, have you, Pop?

Sir Richard   Of course I checked it. My sherry was in it.

Wickerman   We've got the Junior Minister arriving in three minutes, Sir Richard.

Sir Richard   Helga, you are absolutely sure you . . .

Helga   Definitely, Pop. Oh no. You aren't going to have to resign, are you?

Sir Richard   Resign? Certainly not. Battenbergs never resign. I know, we'll get Miss Dobbs to nip over to Companies House. There's usually something or other there.

Wickerman   Sir Richard, that's not going to help us. What have we got now, two more minutes . . .

Helga   Look, Dad, all you have to do is remember what was in it. You can remember, can't you?

Helga *sits down at the table and grabs a notepad.*

Sir Richard   Yes. Well, no. Not in pernickety detail. What about you, Wickerman?

Wickerman   Maybe the odd thing.

Helga   I think you'd both better try. Just a few headings. And I'll write it down. Right, the Kubinski project. Nature of business?

Sir Richard   Good question.

Wickerman   High-rise buildings and property development.

Helga   Capital funding?

Sir Richard   Not very sure.

Wickerman   Shall we say forty million?

Helga   Financial backers?

Sir Richard   Battenberg's Bank.

Wickerman   In consultation with Jurgen Fabry.

Helga   Main projects?

Sir Richard   Ah. Naturally there must have been some.

Wickerman   Wasn't it private and public housing in Greenwich Marshes?

Sir Richard Not sure we should let on too much about Greenwich Marshes.

Helga Better something than nothing. Greenwich Marshes.

Froggatt *comes in.*

Froggatt Sir Richard, Lord Fabry and the Minister are coming up in the lift.

Sir Richard What do we do?

Helga Just play it cool, Pop. Now we've got the file.

The lift pings. In the corridor, the **Beadle** *appears, leading the Junior Minister,* **Mortimer Fitzroy**, *dry and pushy, and the banker,* **Hans Fabry**, *cool and jovial. They come in.* **Wickerman** *goes over to* **Fitzroy** *and leads him over to* **Sir Richard**.

Wickerman May I introduce Mr Mortimer Fitzroy, Sir Richard?

Fitzroy Junior Minister, Deputy PM's department.

Sir Richard Sir Richard Battenberg. Chairman of this ancient bank, for my sins. Delighted, Minister.

Fabry *has gone over to* **Helga**.

Fabry Ah, Helga. What are you doing here? Don't tell me you've joined the team of this august bank.

Helga Not yet. But I am thinking about it, Mr Fabry. It's getting to be career time . . .

Fabry Stephen sends his love. Says he's been missing you.

Helga Thanks. Tell him I've kept on missing him too.

Fitzroy May I just say I'm lunching today at Number 10 with Yasser Arafat. So I do hope we can proceed with great expedition.

Sir Richard Right, Froggatt, call in the board members. You're not thinking of staying, are you, Helga?

Helga I think I'd better, don't you, Pop? You might just need to consult my file on the Kubinski business.

Fitzroy   Ah, the Kubinski business, that reminds me. You may have heard Mr Heseltine's office has been undergoing major administrative reorganization and streamlining?

Sir Richard   Jolly good.

Fitzroy   It's had one or two knock-on effects. Some of our backwork has become temporarily unavailable. Including the, er, Kubinski file.

Sir Richard   You mean you've lost it?

Fitzroy   Not at all. I mean on a temporary basis it happens to be technically unavailable.

Fabry   Which reminds me, Dickie. As you know the technologization of global banking has accelerated so quickly lately that information dispersal and retrieval has been getting severely backlogged.

Sir Richard   So you've lost it too.

Fitzroy   I'm sure Mr Fabry and myself are fully apprized of the issues.

Fabry   Absolutely.

Fitzroy   But it does mean we look forward to your detailed briefing with great interest.

Sir Richard   Good. Excellent. Well, shall we all sit down, gentlemen, Helga . . .

By now the board members have gathered at their places round the table. **Maybelle** *is there to work the projector.* **Helga**, **Froggatt** *also at the table.* **Sir Richard** *takes his seat at the head.*

Sir Richard   Wickerman, you'd better sit here on my right hand.

Wickerman   Yes, sir, I think I probably should.

He sits beside **Sir Richard**.

Sir Richard   Well, gentlemen . . . and young lady . . . we've called this meeting to discuss our mutual commitment to the er . . .

Several   Kubinski project.

Sir Richard   Mr Fabry is here to represent our long-standing partnership.

Fabry   Shortly to be cemented even more positively, eh, Helga?

Helga *tosses her head, not looking too pleased.*

Sir Richard   And we welcome the Minister from the DPM's office. Which has expressed great interest in this exciting and innovative, er, project. Mr Wickerman, would you kindly take us through it?

Paston-Jones *rises and raises a hand.*

Paston-Jones   Excuse me, Chairman. I would like to point out that although Mr Wickerman is making this presentation, the original Kubinski project was initiated by the older board members present. I'd like that clearly understood.

Fenton   I think that might be made clearer if we were to see the file on the original Kubinski project.

Fitzroy   Quite agree.

Helga   I've got it here, Mr Wickerman.

Helga *hands the document to* **Maybelle**, *who shows it on the projector. It's a few handwritten notes on one sheet. All stare at the screen.*

Fitzroy   That's, er, it, Sir Richard?

Sir Richard   Yes. That seems to sum it up. In a nutshell.

Fitzroy   A rather small nutshell. You don't exactly go in for a lot of documentation at Battenberg's, do you?

Sir Richard   Banking discretion. Client confidentiality. That's the heart and soul of merchant banking, Minister. Eh, Fabry?

Fabry   Quite. They may call us old-fashioned. But let it be said, when the story of the City is written, we were always discreet. What isn't written down may never be called to account. Still, could Wickerman . . . maybe flesh it out a little?

Sir Richard   Let's have more flesh, can we?

Wickerman   Certainly. Can we have the next transparency, Miss Dobbs?

Onscreen, a picture of a tower block.

This was one of the Kubinski buildings when it was put up in the sixties.

Lord Holbeck   Ah, remember it well.

Onscreen, a picture of a tower block falling down.

Wickerman   And this is the same building when it fell down in the seventies.

Onscreen, a newspaper headline saying FALLING TOWERS: THE KUBINSKI ENQUIRY REPORTS.

This is coverage of . . .

Fitzroy *rises.*

Fitzroy   The public enquiry. Thank you, Sir Richard, I think I've seen quite enough. Can someone call my car for Number 10?

Fabry *rises.*

Fabry   And on the way could you drop me at the Garrick?

Wickerman   Minister, I was simply showing you Kubinski Mark 1. But the reason for our meeting today is to consider Kubinski Mark 2. Minister, if you wouldn't mind . . .

Fitzroy *and* **Fabry** *unwillingly sit down again.*

Fitzroy   Oh, very well . . .

Onscreen, a picture of a dilapidated building site.

Wickerman   This is the site still owned by Kubinski Holdings.

Onscreen a photo of the Thames.

This is the River Thames.

Onscreen a photo of Greenwich, with Observatory.

This is Greenwich, the home of Mean Time.

Onscreen, a portrait of a group of European leaders.

This is the European Community.

Onscreen a photo of four white horses.

This is the Millennium.

Onscreen a photo of a hand pointing out of the sky.

This is the National Lottery.

The board members look at each other.

Sir Richard   Is any of this relevant, Wickerman?

Wickerman   The nub of the new Kubinski project is to put all these together. The Kubinski site, the Thames at Greenwich, the Millennium, the National Lottery, the EC. Not to say Battenberg's, Jurgen Fabry, and the DTI.

Fitzroy   You've completely lost me, Wickerman.

Onscreen a picture of a glossy hi-tech domed city in glass, very futuristic.

Wickerman   This is the indoor city of the future. You could call it Future City. Call it Technopolis. We build it on the Kubinski site. Which is in the middle of the Millennium exhibition. Which should give us access to private and public investment, Millennium funding, perhaps a grant from the EC, together with matching funding from your department, Minister.

Fitzroy   Just a minute. Let me be quite clear about this. You do own this site, do you, Sir Richard?

Sir Richard   I think so. Don't we?

Wickerman   Battenberg and Jurgen Fabry between them have now acquired all existing stock in Kubinski Holdings. Which includes the title to this site. Naturally if this project went forward, the bank would want to commit to a substantial investment. I think we're talking a hundred million from Battenberg's. Aren't we, Sir Richard?

Sir Richard A hundred . . . ?

Helga Pop.

Sir Richard Well, why not?

Wickerman And a similar sum from your bank, Mr Fabry?

Fabry *shuffles in his chair.*

Fabry Well, we've always been able to match Battenberg's . . .

Wickerman *turns to the Minister.*

Wickerman So, Minister, that's two hundred million from private funding toward a prestigious adventure that will carry Britain into the twenty-first century. Lift the national mood. Relieve unemployment. Show the country its doing something, when most of the time it looks as though it's doing sod all. The Kubinski project is nothing less than the spirit of national renewal.

Fabry European renewal.

Sir Richard Global renewal.

Lord Holbeck And opportunities to celebrate the Millennium don't come along every day of the week.

Paston-Jones No, I'd say they come along roughly once every thousand years, Lord Holbeck.

Fitzroy Reassure me. There's absolutely no way this could turn into a political banana skin, is there, Sir Richard?

Sir Richard Political banana skin? Course not. The bank's been working on it for years. It has our good name behind it. The whole thing's as solid as a er . . .

Wickerman Rock, sir?

Fitzroy Well, in that case, I have indeed been bidden by my Senior Minister to offer you matching funding.

Helga *gets up and goes to him.*

Helga   But that's a bit mean, isn't it? Only two hundred million. For the best development scheme in Britain since the Great Exhibition. And the perfect way to ring in the new Millennium.

Fitzroy   I think it's a massive investment, Miss Battenberg, given our economic problems. Add Millennial Funding. Add investment in infrastructure. Add a development bid to the European Community for aid to a deprived area. I'd say you have to be looking at a total budget of something like three quarters of a billion. Now then, may I go and have couscous with Mr Arafat?

Delight all round.

Sir Richard   Thank you, Minister.

Maybelle   I'll come and see you to your car, Minister.

Fitzroy *and* **Maybelle** *go off. The board stares at* **Wickerman**. **Helga** *starts a round of applause, which is gradually taken up round the table.*

Sir Richard   Quite magnificent, Wickerman.

Fabry   Congratulations. I'm delighted to work with you. And so pleased to see my prospective daughter-in-law turning into a real banker.

Helga   Don't count on it, Mr Fabry.

Fabry *goes.*

Sir Richard   There's a bottle of champagne in my suite. If the partners would care to . . .

The board members head for the boardroom.

Lord Holbeck   The fella used to work in my office once.

Fenton   I took him to White's.

Paston-Jones (*still stunned*)   Three quarters of a billion?

The board off. **Wickerman** *throws his fist in the air.* **Helga** *makes her way over and embraces him. He looks at* **Froggatt**.

Wickerman   Frog, we're there. You couldn't just lend me ten quid, could you? I'd like to take Helga out for a pizza.

Froggatt *reaches for his wallet.*

Froggatt   Here then. This is really your lucky day, Wickers. I'm lending you twenty.

Wickerman   Thanks, you oink . . .

Wickerman *and* **Helga** *go, a happy pair.* **Froggatt** *onstage.*

Froggatt   Bloody bloody Wickerman . . .

Act Three

Six months later.

*The stage area has now become, in effect, **Wickerman**'s office. Same doors off, but now the conference table is loaded with papers and architectural drawings. Centre stage is a large model of the Kubinski project – which takes the form of a domed city with great towers of buildings, walkways, etc. **Wickerman** is talking to a **Journalist**, who has a tape-recorder whirring. Maybe a photographer takes pictures.*

Journalist So what we're looking at now is the architectural model of Future City?

Wickerman That's the scheme that won the international competition. Of course all the world's leading architects put in. Richard Rogers and Norman Foster. Philippe Starck and I. M. Pei. But we decided to go for a design that wasn't just another set of drab post-modern buildings. We're thinking post-post-modern. Radical innovation. Visionary investment in the super-technologies of the twenty-first century.

Journalist So that's why you chose Disney? And what does Prince Charles have to say?

Wickerman He says he's far too busy with domestic matters to comment. See, here's the Virtual Reality Hotel. The Mean Time Internet Café. The Pocahontas Terrace. Treasure Island. And this is the Kubinski Tower. When that's completed, it will be the tallest building in Europe . . .

Journalist You really have secured all the funding, have you, Mr Wickerman? I mean, this isn't going to turn into another Eurotunnel?

Wickerman Funding's all in place. It's not just government. This is backed by Battenberg's Bank, remember. Where your security is our confidence.

Journalist   Right, Mr Wickerman. Oh, just one more question. Who is Kubinski?

Wickerman   Who is . . . Kubinski?

Journalist   It's called the Kubinski project. You're erecting the Kubinski Tower, Europe's tallest building. I take it somewhere behind all this there's a Mr Kubinski? And didn't this all start with a company called Kubinski Holdings?

Wickerman   There's a company called Virgin. That doesn't mean there's a Virgin somewhere.

Journalist   But there is a Richard Branson.

Wickerman   Yes, there definitely is a Richard Branson. It's just a name, isn't it? It might be anything. But it happens to be Kubinski.

Froggatt *appears at the door. His clothes have improved and he has a mobile phone to his ear.*

Froggatt (*phone*)   Yes, Jed . . . Leave it with me, I'll get back to you on that one soonest. Don't do anything I wouldn't do. That should give you a pretty free hand, hoink hoink . . . OK, sunbeam, *ciao*.

Wickerman   Do you mind, Mr Froggatt?

Froggatt   Sorry, Mr Wickerman. Didn't know you were doing an interview. The site engineer wants you to get down to Greenwich to look at claddings.

Journalist   Don't worry. That should look splendid on the front pages. I think I've everything I need.

The lift pings. **Journalist** *goes,* **Fenton** *enters – now a bitter man.*

Fenton   So, this is the famous model, is it? Isn't it all a little bit vulgar?

Wickerman   Well, you are looking at the twenty-first century, Mr Fenton.

Fenton   Talking to journalists? Is that wise, Wickerman? I see the papers have been having a go at you.

Wickerman   Have they? What for?

Fenton   Usual thing. Who is this man? What's his background? Doesn't look like one of us.

Wickerman   I suppose that's what the financial pages are there for. And selling tricky pension schemes.

Fenton   It's always the same. Most city financiers get called sharks by the press at some time or other. Problem is, some of them are, aren't they? Oh, by the way, I see the Opposition are raising some rather nasty questions in the House. Sir Richard about?

Wickerman   He's in his office. He came in very early this month. I didn't know he was expecting you, Mr Fenton. He didn't say anything to me.

Fenton   No, he wouldn't, would he? You see, he's called a special partners' meeting about Kubinski. To review progress. Make sure everything's in good order. Counter any questions of scandal or impropriety. We wouldn't want anything to tarnish the good name of Battenberg's, would we?

Wickerman   No, Mr Fenton. Not again.

Fenton *goes into the office.*

Wickerman   What was all that about?

Froggatt   I think Fenton's fantastically jealous of you, Wickers. He doesn't trust you. I can't think why . . . but for some reason he suspects you're the kind of man who would angle for his job.

Maybelle *comes in, followed by* **Paston-Jones** *and* **Holbeck**.

Maybelle   Sir Richard got in very early this morning. I think you should both proceed straight in.

Paston-Jones   Morning, gentlemen, morning. Just been reading about you in the papers, Wickerman.

Lord Holbeck *halts at the model.*

Lord Holbeck   Great Scott, what's all this?

Wickerman   The City of the Future, Lord Holbeck.

Lord Holbeck   Yes, thought I remembered it.

Paston-Jones *and* **Holbeck** *are shown into the Chairman's suite. The lift pings and* **Helga** *comes in.*

Wickerman   Helga. Why have you come here?

Helga   I simply had to see the model. Is that it?

Wickerman   There it is. What do you think?

Helga   I think it's brilliant. And it's all you. Your dream city. I can hardly wait to live in it.

Wickerman   I'd like to live in it with you. Been seeing much of Stephen Fabry lately?

Helga   I'm completely over and out with Stephen. He will keep going to the opera.

Wickerman   I know. I will keep sending him tickets.

Helga   You never go to the opera. You steal other people's picnics and have a good time outside.

Wickerman   How perfectly you understand me.

Helga   Well, I could get to understand you even better. Oh, can't you just go away, Froggie? We'd like to be head to head for a minute or two.

Froggatt   At it again, Wickers?

The door to the Chairman's suite opens and the board members appear.

Sir Richard   Froggatt, just a second, little job for you. I want you to slip down to Personnel Department and bring up Mr Wickerman's file. Find it this time.

Wickerman *reacts anxiously.*

Wickerman   Hold it, Froggie. Did you say, bring up my . . . file, Sir Richard? May I ask why?

Sir Richard   Yes, Tim. I've been thinking over the weekend.

Paston-Jones   No better time for it.

Sir Richard   Go on, Froggatt, don't just stand there. Go and dig out that file . . .

Froggatt *looks at* **Wickerman**, *goes*. **Sir Richard** *claps his hands for attention*.

Sir Richard   Now, gentlemen, Helga, can I have your attention? Battenberg's, you know, is a proud and ancient bank. Old-fashioned in some ways. Very far-seeing in others. It's always changed with the times. When the Eiffel Tower was erected in, er . . .

Paston-Jones   Paris . . .

Sir Richard   In 1889, Battenberg's put up much of the financing.

Lord Holbeck   I remember.

Sir Richard   And when, a few years later, the London underground railway was laid, it was once again Battenberg's who raised most of the capital. Which is why I often like to say that ours is a bank that has always had its ups and downs . . .

Fenton   Yes, Chairman.

Sir Richard   . . . and why it can confidently claim to have played its part in the making of the twentieth century. But nothing in my own time of office here has made me prouder than the sight that greets my eyes today. There it is, gentlemen. Future City.

Clapping from the board.

Once more we take our place in the technological and commercial front line. My friends, we can all claim a hand in this triumph . . .

Fenton   Quite so, sir.

Paston-Jones   Every single one of us.

Sir Richard   But one person above all has had the imagination and, yes, the courage to see this adventure through.

Helga   Hear hear.

Sir Richard   One young man on our team has carried the whole thing from initial foreplay to conception, then to full term and whatever should happen to lie beyond. You all know who I mean. I mean, er . . .

Helga   Tim Wickerman, Dad.

Sir Richard   I mean exactly that, Tim Wickerman. So, Tim, presuming the consent of the partners and the board, which I'm supremely confident I have, I intend to recognize your sterling service. I'm going to make you our new Chief Executive.

Helga   Brilliant. Bring on the Golden Handcuffs!

The board members look far from enthusiastic.

Fenton   Sorry, Sir Richard. I'm the Chief Executive.

Sir Richard   Quite so. I may not be a hands-on Chairman, but I'd not overlooked that. I propose to relieve you of that tedious duty and make you a full partner in the bank. And to raise your share of bonuses. And to put you up for the Cottesmore.

Fenton   Very kind of you. But I do think I should have been consulted first.

Paston-Jones   The fact is, Chairman, it's a board matter. We should all have been consulted first.

Lord Holbeck   I'm trying to remember whether I was consulted.

Fenton   Surely before we set this in stone it should go before a full meeting of the partners?

Sir Richard   Gentlemen, may I remind you that this is a family bank? Battenbergs have always run it. And now that my daughter is showing such a keen interest, I have every hope that Battenbergs always will.

Helga   You can bet your bonus on it, Dad.

The board members look at each other.

Paston-Jones   It's an important decision. Personally I know very little about Wickerman's educational background, or his banking experience. Frankly, it's not at all clear to me he's actually one of us.

Fenton   There've been some very strange stories in the press just lately . . .

Helga   I wonder where they came from?

A discussion rises, **Wickerman** *interrupts.*

Wickerman   If you don't mind me saying so, Sir Richard, I wasn't consulted either. I do realize this is a very great honour. But the truth is I don't actually want to be your Chief Executive.

Fenton   Why don't you want to be CEO? What the devil's wrong with it?

Helga   Of course you want to be Chief Executive. I want you to be Chief Executive.

Sir Richard   Do I see something in the romantic direction developing here?

Wickerman   I really mean it, Sir Richard.

Sir Richard   Oh, I assure you your salary will be significantly regraded. And in the upward direction.

Wickerman   I don't want any more salary either.

Sir Richard   And we'll increase your bonuses.

Wickerman   I'm not interested in your bonuses.

Paston-Jones   But that's absurd. Unheard of in the City.

Hubbub rises. **Wickerman** *turns to* **Maybelle**.

Wickerman   So, Miss Dobbs, could you please ring down to Personnel at once and tell Froggatt to forget about bringing up my file?

Maybelle *goes to her office.*

Sir Richard   Now look here, Wickerman. I know my own mind. I reward talent when I see it. And I never take no for an answer. Unless no's the answer I want.

A beat.

Wickerman   All right, Sir Richard. Then there's something I'd better tell you before this goes any further. Things in this bank are not quite what they seem.

Sir Richard   They're exactly what they seem.

Helga   I'm not sure this is such a great idea, Tim.

Wickerman   As you're all aware, over the six months I've been up here in top office I've worked extremely hard for the bank.

Sir Richard   Absolutely. And you can see now it's not gone unnoticed.

Wickerman   But there's one small thing you don't seem to have noticed. The fact is, I'm not actually on the staff of Batttenberg's at all.

Paston-Jones   What do you mean, not on the staff?

Wickerman   You see, I just . . . sort of came in one day. Got myself a desk over there. Started doing a bit of trading. But I never did have a job as such. I mean, I never had an interview. Never had a contract. Never had a salary. So if anyone in the bank should ever get curious enough actually to check the accounts, they'd find you never paid me a penny.

The board members stare at him.

Fenton   You mean, you're a total impostor?

Wickerman   Not really an impostor. Because that means you're impersonating someone, and I wasn't impersonating anyone. I was just being me, really. You had this big old merchant bank show going, and I just sort of joined in.

Paston-Jones   And what about the Kubinski project?

Wickerman   Well, once I was here I had to do something, didn't I?

Sir Richard *stares at him.*

Sir Richard   You had to do something. And just what did you do, Wickerman?

Wickerman   Well, I simply found this dead company in the computer no one was doing anything with. To start with, it was just . . . practice really. Then I got a bit of trading going. Then I got some competitive interest and that drove up the price. Then I got the Ministry involved. And everything else sort of snowballed on from there.

The board members look at each other and him.

Fenton   But who actually authorized this trading?

Wickerman   Well, Sir Richard kindly signed all the necessary documents.

Fenton   And who in back office checked it?

Wickerman   Well, I did. Because I happened to be here already, you see. I was able to be back to my front and front to my back.

Fenton   And I presume ever since then you've been living high on the profits?

Wickerman   Not really. I've never seen any. Only on paper.

Fenton   You know what this is? Ring dealing. Fraudulent management. Rat trading.

Sir Richard   Rat trading?

Fenton   It's criminal. It's illegal. The whole thing's a fraud from start to finish.

Sir Richard   Is it, Wickerman?

Wickerman   I wouldn't call it a fraud, Sir Richard. I've taken nothing for myself. Except for the Porsche.

Sir Richard   What would you call it then?

Wickerman Creative banking.

Helga You see, banking and business are all based on an illusion, aren't they?

Wickerman Exactly. It's fiction. A big dream.

Helga A wonderful dream, Dad. Look at it.

Paston-Jones The trouble is you've been dreaming with other people's investments. Other people's honour and reputation. Other people's cash.

Fenton Our cash.

Paston-Jones It's rogue trading. And if there were any justice in this world you would go to prison for a very long time.

Lord Holbeck In my day any decent man who found himself in Wickerman's position would have gone out and hanged himself. With a very apologetic note.

Fenton I think the least you can do now is clear out your desk and get out of this building at once.

Helga Don't you think all this is totally unfair?

Sir Richard Helga. Do you know something about this?

Helga I do, actually. And I can't see what the fuss is about.

Fenton You can't see what the fuss is about?

Helga This is the City of London, isn't it? You're gentlemen, and you protect each other. But you've done nothing for Tim at all. You haven't even had the decency to pay him a penny.

Paston-Jones How could we pay him? On paper the man doesn't exist. He's a fiction too.

Helga Pop, you said the bank had had its ups and downs. There've been a lot of downs lately, haven't there? This rogue trader in Hong Kong, where you lost millions? Because you were all too complacent to keep an eye on the accounts?

Sir Richard   There has been a short-term liquidity problem, yes.

Helga   You mean you've been ordered to pay back thirty million to investors. But Tim hasn't cheated you. In fact he's saved you. With this brilliant Kubinski project. The City of the Future.

They all turn and look again at the model.

A multi-million pound reality. There it is. Look at it. See what he's done. And if you were to expose Tim, or report him, or fire him . . .

Sir Richard   I'm not sure that's technically possible. Since we never knowingly employed him in the first place . . .

Helga   . . . or if he just left, you'd still be dependent on the profits he'd brought you. Which sounds pretty ucky to me. And supposing he were to go to authorities and confess what he'd done? What would happen to the bank? It would crash, wouldn't it? This whole ancient and noble edifice would disappear. Right down the loo.

Lord Holbeck   Funny, you know. Always knew I didn't remember him.

Sir Richard *stares at her.*

Sir Richard   Gentlemen, it looks to me like serious thinking time.

Wickerman   Let me save you the trouble of thinking. I know how hard it is for all of you. I'm going. I created your City of the Future. These are the thanks I get.

Sir Richard   Now wait a minute, Wickerman.

Fenton   I think we should let him go. He should never have been here in the first place. Who brought him in?

Lord Holbeck   Froggatt, I suppose. Never trusted him.

The lift pings, and **Froggatt** *comes in, a large file under his arm.*

Paston-Jones   Ah, there you are, Froggatt. Come and sit down. You've got some serious explaining to do.

Froggatt   Yes, I know, sir. I'm sorry it took so long. But I had a lot of difficulty finding Mr Wickerman's personnel record.

Fenton   Yes, I bet you did.

Froggatt   Still, there it is. Mr Wickerman's personal file.

A beat.

Sir Richard   His file?

Froggatt   Yes. It seems there's been a computer error. None of his salary cheques has been issued for the last six months. That means he's due to a very large payout.

Fenton   Large payout?

Froggatt   I put the cheque through, it's there in the envelope.

Froggatt *hands* **Sir Richard** *the file. Mystified, he starts leafing through it.*

Sir Richard   Are you now telling me that Mr Wickerman *is* an employee of the bank?

Froggatt   Yes, you can see on the employee roll, sir. And the personnel print-out. He's been with us for the last eighteen months.

Wickerman   I've been with us how long?

Sir Richard   Wickerman, do forgive me for appearing baffled, but that's because I am. You just told us a very long story about how you never actually worked here, even when you did. Now it's quite apparent that you actually were working here, even when you say you really weren't. Can you explain how and why?

Wickerman   Explain? Helga? Frog?

Helga   I expect Tim just pretended he didn't work here because he wanted to be convinced the partners really did trust him.

Froggatt   And valued him not just as another boring name on the payroll but the brilliant and inventive trader he is.

Sir Richard   Is that what it's all been about. Wickerman?

Wickerman   I couldn't have put it better myself.

The partners look at each other.

Paston-Jones   Fact is, all that rigmarole he gave us never took me in for one single second.

Fenton   I was there when he was interviewed for his job in the first place. Saw his promise at once.

Lord Holbeck   And I can remember when he sat over by the window in my office.

Sir Richard   Right, gentlemen. And may I take it on the basis of that show of confidence we now agree Mr Wickerman should become Chief Executive of Battenberg's? With special responsibility for the Kubinski project?

Fenton   Look, why don't we say with *total* responsibility for the Kubinski project?

Paston-Jones   Including any explanations the authorities might at any point require.

Sir Richard   Quite. May I take that as affirmatives all round? Good. Well, congratulations, Wickerman.

Wickerman   I should like to think it over, Sir Richard. You see, once the other banks realize how much I've managed to achieve at Battenberg's, I imagine a lot of the big players will be competing for my services. So it seems to me everything depends on whether we can come to a mutually agreed package on salary, bonus privileges, perks and partnership options. Plus of course pension, life insurance and all analogous benefits.

Helga   It is a Winner Take All world out there.

Sir Richard   Quite understood.

Fenton   On the other hand, if Mr Wickerman can get such remarkable offers, should we be standing in his way?

Sir Richard   Rather good point, Fenton.

Helga   But, Dad, you just can't afford to let him go now, can you? Not if the whole financial future of the bank is in his hands? You're just going to have to lock him in . . .

Sir Richard   Quite so, my dear. Look, I think the partners had better come into my suite and we'll discuss this contract right away. Over a hastily convened glass of sherry . . .

Lord Holbeck   Wondered when we'd get to the sherry.

The board members go, leaving **Wickerman** *with* **Froggatt** *and* **Helga**. **Wickerman** *looks at his cheque.*

Wickerman   Three hundred thousand?

Froggatt   And bonuses to come.

Helga   And a top-flight contract. It's just brill, darling.

Wickerman   And you're brill, Froggie. But what were you doing downstairs just now?

Froggatt   It's all your fault, Wickers. I never committed a fraudulent act in my entire life until today.

Wickerman   Fed me into the files, did you?

Froggatt   Just tapped you in, Wickerman. I accessed you. Except to access isn't really a verb.

Helga   Isn't he terrific? Good old Frog.

She kisses him.

Wickerman   Froggie, it's truly noble of you. But old Felstedians always stick together, eh?

Froggatt   Oh, it wasn't that. I never really liked you, Wickers. You made me do your homework. You took everything you could off me. And you always pulled the birds.

Helga   Still does, don't you, Timmy?

Wickerman   But in that case why . . .

Froggatt   For one thing I'm very tidy, you see. I just couldn't bear the thought of working every day with an employee whose details weren't recorded in the files.

Wickerman *puts an arm round him.*

Wickerman   Anyway, thanks, Froggie. Only one thing I don't quite understand. You said I'd been working here for the last eighteen months. And I've only not been working here for the last six.

Froggatt   Well, it wasn't easy. You see, I had to attach your name to the records of someone who'd already been working for Battenberg's.

Helga   Who's that?

Froggatt   Oh, someone who'd been trading for us in the Pacific and recently left the bank. So that's who you are, Wickers.

Maybelle *appears from* **Sir Richard***'s suite.*

Maybelle   Can you come in now, Mr Wickerman?

Wickerman *goes.* **Helga** *looks at* **Froggatt**.

Helga   Not the one Interpol are after?

Froggatt   Yes, as a matter of fact.

Helga   Isn't that clever, Froggie?

Froggatt   Yes, isn't it?

The lift pings. In the corridor the **Beadle** *appears leading* **Fitzroy**, *the Junior Minister. They come in.* **Maybelle** *reappears.*

Beadle   Mr Fitzroy the Junior Minister has arrived, Mr Froggatt. And given his highly prestigious status I thought I should show him straight up.

Froggatt   Quite right, Bennett. Excuse me, I just have to make a phone call.

Froggatt *goes into* **Maybelle***'s office. The* **Beadle** *leaves.*

Fitzroy   Look, I need to see Sir Richard at once. And it really won't wait. I'm due to confront our formidable Prime Minister in twenty minutes' time.

Maybelle   He's contractually head to head with the partners, Minister. But I'll ask him to step out.

Fitzroy   In fact you'd better ask all of them to step out.
This is extremely serious.

Maybelle   Yes, Minister.

Wickerman *comes out of the Chairman's suite.*

Wickerman   There isn't some sort of . . . problem, is
there?

Fitzroy   Oh yes there is. About Government funding for
your bloody Future City thing. You could be in for a real
Millennium, Wickerman. With plagues of locusts.
Garnished with sun-dried boils and a side-plate of four white
horsemen.

*He indicates the model. The board members appear from the
Chairman's suite.*

Sir Richard   Morning, Minister, how can we help? I
presume this is about the Kubinski project?

Fitzroy   Yes, it is. And I suggest we all sit down,
gentlemen. Because I have something of considerable
moment to say.

Sir Richard   Oh dear.

All present sit round the conference table, and turn their attention to
Fitzroy, *who begins handing papers out round the table.* **Maybelle**
distributes them.

Fitzroy   Naturally, given the massive amount of
taxpayers' money we proposed to commit to the project,
we've had teams of lawyers combing all through the
documentation. After all, we're not noted for spending
public money extravagantly, are we?

Sir Richard   You're not noted for spending it at all.
Anyway, I'm sure they'll find everything in order. Oh, come
and sit down, Froggatt.

Froggatt *has reappeared from* **Maybelle***'s office.*

Fitzroy   Are you? I'm hoping you can reassure me.
Because very shortly I'm going to have to go and reassure the

Prime Minister. Since our team have drawn one very worrying fact to my attention.

Fenton (*smoothly*)   I think it might be useful at this stage to point out that our new Chief Executive, Mr Wickerman, is solely responsible for the Kubinski affair.

Paston-Jones   Totally. In every detail.

Fitzroy   Our team's been doing due diligence and working through the fine print. They note that for some reason one interested party has been totally omitted from the Kubinski project. I mean Mr Peter Kubinski.

Sir Richard   Oh, is that all?

Fitzroy   Is there an explanation?

Sir Richard   Oh, yes, there's an explanation. Mr Kubinski is no longer traceable.

Fitzroy   Really? Why not?

Paston-Jones   There was a public enquiry and he went bankrupt. This was long ago, of course. But that's how we acquired his stock.

Sir Richard   After that, he was supposed to have left the country for South America. I suppose he thought discretion was the better part of valour.

Lord Holbeck   According to my memory, he's dead. Or was that Martin Bormann?

Fitzroy   Martin Bormann? Don't say he was involved too?

Sir Richard   Minister, all this is in the past. It can't affect our government funding. Can it?

Fitzroy   Of course it can. Sir Richard, no government could be more committed than ours to the twenty-first century. We've been behind it from the beginning. But there are more important things. Like negative press publicity and questions in the house. After all, as the PM reminded me at six thirty this morning, when I was still in the bath, the one thing this present government will definitely not stand for is sleaze.

Sir Richard   And he'll find the City of London behind him every step of the way. But exactly what do you want us to do?

Fitzroy   Do? Don't you see what we could be staring in the face? Kubinskigate. One false move and there'll be Nolans and Tumins and Caldicotts all over the place. Followed by long fraud trials, weeping pensioners, questions in the House, and calls for my head on a platter. What we must do, gentlemen, is establish all the facts. And then decide whether we want to reveal them or not.

Sir Richard   Or not?

Fitzroy   The golden rule is full and frank disclosure. Hide nothing. Unless you're totally sure that no one can dig it up. The question is, is Kubinski a dead duck? Or is he a smoking gun?

Lord Holbeck   How would we know?

Fitzroy   Surely there's a proper record of him in your original files?

Sir Richard   Minister, you already saw the original files.

Fitzroy   You mean that tacky piece of paper that could have been scribbled down in ten minutes?

Froggatt   I think it was three, actually.

Wickerman (*kicks him*)   Froggie, you dipstick . . .

Fitzroy   Where exactly are the original files?

Fenton   Wickerman started this. He must have had the original files.

Wickerman   I gave them to Miss Battenberg . . .

Helga   I gave them to you, Pop.

Sir Richard   I really don't remember.

Lord Holbeck   Nor do I.

Fitzroy   How very convenient.

Froggatt   Actually, Minister, I think I can help a little here. I found the original files. But I shredded them.

They all stare at him.

Fitzroy   To abet in a cover-up?

Froggatt   Certainly not, sir. Mr Wickerman is such a remarkable man I didn't want anything to embarrass him.

Fitzroy   So we'll never trace Kubinski? Find his title? Get his consent?

Froggatt   'Fraid not, sir. Does that mean Wickerman should never have been trading in that company in the first place?

Fitzroy *rises and gathers up his papers.*

Fitzroy   Of course it does. That's it, gentlemen. I shall inform the Prime Minister of what happened at this meeting. And I think you can now say a firm goodbye to your absurd City of the Future . . .

He's just about to leave when the lift pings. The **Old Man** *we have seen before comes in and goes centre stage, pursued by the* **Beadle**.

Beadle   You can't go in there, sir, there's a crown minister present. Sorry, gents, just couldn't stop him.

Sir Richard   What is it?

Old Man   I just want a word with the Chairman.

Wickerman   Now come on, old fella, you know you're not allowed up here. Let me take you downstairs.

Wickerman *is about to lead the* **Old Man** *out, and make his own escape . . .*

Sir Richard   Just a minute. You stay there, Wickerman. Now, what do you want?

Wickerman   He just wants to shine your shoes, Sir Richard. Let's go, come along . . .

Old Man   I've been trying to have a word with you for months, Sir Richard. My name's Kubinski.

Sir Richard *and the board members react.*

Sir Richard   Eh? Did you say Kubinski?

Fitzroy   Yes, did you?

Old Man   Peter Kubinski, why not? Of Kubinski Personal
Valeting Services for Commercial Gentlemen. But I see
you're not interested, sir, so I'll . . .

Sir Richard   Just a minute. You wouldn't be Kubinski of
Kubinski Holdings?

Old Man   I did have a company once. Wasn't much good
though. Some dreadful sharks got hold of it, and declared me
bankrupt.

Fitzroy   So you fled to South America?

Old Man   I took a two-week holiday in the Seychelles. And
rethought my life . . .

Sir Richard *exudes bonhomie.*

Sir Richard   Well, Mr Kubinski, I do believe we have
some rather good news for you.

Old Man   You do want your shoes shined?

Sir Richard   Not quite. We'd like to invite you to join our
Board of Directors. Wouldn't we, gentlemen?

Warm agreement all round.

Old Man   Board of Directors?

Paston-Jones   We'd be delighted to make you a partner.

Old Man   Of the great bank of Battenberg's?

Sir Richard   I'd gladly put you up for the Cottesmore.

Paston-Jones   And I'll back you for Boodles.

Old Man   Oh no. I'm not sure I'd want to, at my age. Bank
partners, I know what happens to them. Some of my best
clients write me letters from jail. I think I'll stick to
something safer. You're sure you don't want your shoes
shined?

Sir Richard   Look, man, the future of the bank's at stake.

Fitzroy *steps forward.*

Fitzroy   Mr Kubinski, I represent the Deputy Prime Minister. You understand? And I'm sure he'd want to say that, if you were to do us the favour of joining Battenberg's, you'd probably do a great deal to help keep this government in office.

Old Man   Oh dear. That's a terrible responsibility.

Wickerman   Not just that. If you joined the board, you could help create the wonderful world of the twenty-first century.

Old Man   I'm not sure I'd want to be blamed for that either.

Wickerman   See, here, there it is. The City of the Future. You and I, we'll build it on Greenwich Marshes.

He shows the **Old Man** *the model.*

Old Man   Yes, but it would fall down, wouldn't it? Anyone with half an eye can see that.

Sir Richard   Now look, why don't we all retire to my executive suite? And discuss this whole thing over an exceedingly large glass of sherry?

The **Old Man** *heads for the door.*

Old Man   No, Sir Richard, if you don't want personal grooming, I think I'll . . .

Wickerman *grabs him.*

Wickerman   You can have anything. Anything. A silver Porsche. Jemima Goldsmith. Sharon Stone. Now come along, old fella . . .

The directors and **Fitzroy** *lead the protesting* **Old Man** *to* **Sir Richard***'s suite. All go within, with the exception of* **Froggatt** *and the* **Beadle**. **Froggatt** *goes to the cupboard and gets his bicycle wheel.*

Beadle   Not leaving early? Not like you, Mr Froggatt.

Froggatt   Well, it rather looks as if they've settled things here for today.

The **Beadle** *inspects the model on the table.*

Beadle   So they will be getting the City of the Future?

Froggatt   I shouldn't bet on it.

Froggatt *presses the tower that rises from the model. It retracts or collapses. Or maybe it's on a spring and just wobbles alarmingly.*

Beadle   Oh dear, sir. Still, I prefer the past meself. Course, I suppose that's what comes of working forty years at Battenberg's. Makes you a bit . . . traditional.

His mobile phone goes.

Beadle   Scuse me, sir. Really, these things . . . (*Phone.*) Beadle here . . . That's right, love . . . No, I don't imagine he'll be very long, they're finishing . . . So if the gentleman would kindly . . . Right, I'll inform Mr Froggatt.

Froggatt   Anything interesting?

Beadle   There's an Inspector Rattle downstairs.

Froggatt   Oh yes? The man from Interpol?

Beadle   Yes, sir. He said he wouldn't mind waiting till the meeting was over.

Froggatt   Good. That's exactly what I suggested.

Beadle   Apparently he wants to invite Mr Timothy to fly to Hong Kong with him. He has some outstanding enquiries he thinks Mr Tim can help him with.

Froggatt   Well, who better?

Beadle   That Mr Tim, doesn't he get about? As you said, sir, money doesn't sleep any more . . . I always knew Mr Tim would end up a real high-flyer.

Froggatt   And you were right.

Froggatt *puts on his helmet.* **Helga** *comes out of the boardroom.*

Helga   Frog? You wouldn't care to take me for lunch to Le Gavroche, would you? I was going with Tim. But now they've found Mr Kubinski he thinks he could be detained for quite some time.

Froggatt   Yes, I expect he will be. It is a bit difficult, Helga. I've no money. And I've only got one bicycle.

Helga   My plastic will do nicely, and we'll go in Daddy's limo. Here, Mr Bennett . . .

She grabs the bicycle wheel and hands it to the **Beadle**.

Froggatt   Are you sure about this, Helga?

Helga   Of course I'm sure. I've been watching you, Frog. I always did like a man who was hungry . . .

Helga *and* **Froggatt** *go, the* **Beadle** *follows, and* . . .

End.